GW00367319

100
Best Wel

1000
Best Web Sites

BRUCE DURIE

How To Books

Published by How To Books Ltd, 3 Newtec Place,
Magdalen Road, Oxford OX4 1RE, United Kingdom
Tel: 01865 793806 Fax: 01865 248780
E-mail: info@howtobooks.co.uk
www.howtobooks.co.uk

Reprinted 2000

British Library Cataloguing in Publication Data.
A catalogue record for this book is available from
the British Library.

Edited by Julie Nelson/Cover image PhotoDisc
Cover design by Shireen Nathoo Design

Produced for How To Books by Deer Park Productions
Typeset by PDQ Typesetting, Stoke-on-Trent, Staffs.
Printed and bound in Great Britain

Note: The material contained in this book is set out in good
faith for general guidance and no liability can be accepted for
loss or expense incurred as a result of relying in particular
circumstances on statements made in the book. Laws and
regulations are complex and liable to change, and readers
should check the current position with the relevant
authorities before making personal arrangements.

CONTENTS

CONTENTS

CONTENTS

Special thanks to Joe Palca, Chris Hutchison, Jason Filer, Giles Lewis and Jamie for their contributions.

A BOOK OF WEB SITES?

At first sight a book consisting of web sites might seem counter-intuitive. After all, all web sites are on the web, by definition, so that's the best place to find them. In addition, their addresses and content may change, while the print in a book remains static and can go out of date, but it is worth examining all these points in some detail.

ALL WEB SITES ARE ON THE WEB

That's right – some 30 million of them. So where do you start? Which search engine should you use? How will you know if the web sites you find are worthwhile, informative, well-designed or just a scam? This book aims to give web surfers – especially those new to this engrossing pastime (newbies) or those for whom time is valuable – a filter and a guide, somewhere to start, knowing that some of the hard work and initial scanning has been done for you. There is a section on web search engines and how to get the best from them, and each main section has at least one link to a site of links so you can delve deeper should you wish.

WEB ADDRESSES AND CONTENT CHANGE

Indeed they do. Even bookmarking a favourite site is no guarantee that the URL (Universal Resource Locator – the 'address' of the site) won't change or that the site won't simply get abandoned like a Christmas puppy. There are ways to keep your bookmarks updated, but even this is no defence against the 'dead' or moved site. However, in recognition of this, there is a partner web site to this book http://www.fifeweb.net/1000best/links.htm which will contain the same URLs but in their latest form, which will be updated as often as possible. And in case anyone should think that there is no point buying the book if the listing is freely available – it only contains the links, not any sort of description. However, you could download this file and use it as another Bookmark (for Netscape users) or Favorites (for Internet Explorer) file and set it to update regularly. Full instructions on how to do this are on page 202.

BOOKS CAN GO OUT OF DATE

This book itself will be updated regularly and may contain suggestions from readers – leave your favourite link at http://www.fifeweb.net/1000best/links.htm

If you think books are out-of-date technology, try taking your computer on a train. The great advantage of a book is its portability. It is also an easy-to-use reference source.

Think of this publication rather like a guidebook to an unfamiliar country – why would you need a guidebook when the entire country is before you and all you have to do is travel about in it? But where do you start, what do you look for and where can you get a friendly native to help take the frustration out of the process? And how can you get all of these in a convenient, pocket-sized format?

That's what this book is – your Pocket Guide to the Wonderful World of the Web.

HOW TO USE THIS BOOK

The book is divided into more than 100 sections, each one covering an area of interest. These are rather arbitrarily chosen and you may find something you are looking for in one section rather than another – it was a toss of the coin whether Sports News went into Sports or News and in some cases the decision was to include a particular link in more than one category. At the end of the book is an index of all web sites in the book, arranged alphabetically by nickname. This is so that if you know your favourite site is called Nimby you can refer to the index and find that the main page URL is actually http://www.nimby.net/start/files/choose/index.html which you would never carry around in your head.

WHAT MAKES A GOOD WEB SITE?

A good web site has to be attractive, quick to load, full of interesting content, easy to read, full of exciting links that work and generally make you want to go back to it. A good web site also has a certain something extra – an interesting look, clever implementation, excellent information, something useful for free or just a certain quirkiness that appeals.

But the *best* web site makes you buy something, do something, go somewhere via a link, say 'How did they do that' and – most of all – makes you bookmark it for a revisit. Some you will visit often (say for software information) and some once in a blue moon (like booking that exotic holiday).

This book contains an admittedly personal choice of such sites – some are superbly designed, some are full of useful information, some are clever, some are idiosyncratic and many are all of these. But mainly, they are intended to be useful, provide you with something, act as a good starting point or be instructive in the way they are put together.

DYNAMIC HTML, JAVA AND VERSION 4 BROWSERS

Many new web sites use the latest in web technology. Dynamic HTML is a way of making the web page change according to the user's interaction with it. Java is a programming language that allows the browser to display things that simple HTML can't handle. There are other recent innovations such as ActiveX controls. In the main, these can all be handled by Version 4 browsers – that is, any version of Netscape Navigator or Netscape Communicator above Version 4.0 and any version of Internet Explorer above Version 4. You may need to download specific plug-ins – additional small programs which enable your browser to display certain types of animation, play sound etc. Links to these can be found in the Software and Must Haves sections of this book (pages 31 and 98), as well as download sites for the latest browsers listed above.

There is a great deal of talk about e-business. Most people assume this is the same as e-commerce (selling things via the web or internet) but in fact it is, like marketing or quality, a total business philosophy. And part of it is knowing where, and where best, to find business information on the web. This field is literally endless, since it expands daily, but listed in this section are a few decent places to start.

TAXATION K-BASE   http://www.rroom.co.uk/tkb/index.html

On the web, it is possible to feel like you are one step away from that vital piece of information, but finding it is too time-consuming and frustrating. For this reason, The Reading Room designed K-Base, a powerful, fast search engine for business questions. The Taxation K-Base is a free service with information on and access to courses, self-assessment information, resources for professional tax advisers and an international tax resource database covering more than 100 countries. A truly useful professional resource.

CNNFN   http://cnnfn.com/

CNN's Financial Network is one of the best resources of its kind on the web. There is a special European markets section and links to the Exchanges of
London (http://www.londonstockex.co.uk/),
Frankfurt (http://www.exchange.de/fwb/fwb) and
Paris (http://www.bourse-de-paris.fr/bourse/sbf/homesbf.fcgi?GB).
Elegantly designed and fast to load, this should provide any business with the market information its needs.

FEDEX   http://www.fedex.com

Federal Express would love you to use them for all your shipping and courier needs. Whether you do or not, they have excellent, free software for handling shipping including the FedEx World Tracking Software and a comprehensive shipping package. These multi-lingual Windows-based programs provide real-time tracking information, a world map for routing, laser-printing of shipping documents and reports and more. A good business resource in its own right.

DEPARTMENT OF TRADE AND INDUSTRY   http://www.dti.gov.uk/

The DTI site has a wealth of information on business support, regulations and competitiveness, made available via an excellent search engine. There is also an on-line complaints procedure. The design is clear, calm and uncluttered.

THE ENTERPRISE ZONE   http://www.enterprisezone.org.uk/

EZ is a UK gateway to business information on the web for everyone who is in business in the United Kingdom, developed by Microsoft with the Business Link community and the DTI (see above). It has a good search engine for finding web sites for businesses of all sizes, whether start up or high growth. The DTI rather missed their chance to provide meaningful and practical management materials and tools. But a truly comprehensive and well-thought-out listing, some of which were also by the DTI, can be found on the wholly excellent Bnet (http://www.bnet.co.uk).

THE ECONOMIST   http://www.economist.co.uk/

The seminal business weekly has an excellent on-line presence. There are different levels of access if you register or subscribe, but a great deal is available free. Registration gives access to archive information which is usually pay-to-download. One of the surprising aspects of The Economist is the depth and authority of its science and technology coverage.

BUSINESSMAN'S GUIDE TO EUROPE
http://europa.eu.int/en/comm/dg23/guide_en/index2.htm

Bewildered by Europe? Wondering what help is out there? Where are all the lucrative EU contracts, grants and projects? All is revealed in this site. There is also a link to other EU Member State official sites (http://europa.eu.int/en/comm/dg23/smesites/eu_state.htm) and an excellent search engine.

HOOVER'S UK
http://www.hoovers.co.uk/

Hoover's has provided information on US companies for decades and recently opened this UK-focused site for business information. The database contains over 13,500 companies world-wide. There are also news headlines, a careers and jobs section and other useful items including a good list of government information sites.

HM TREASURY
http://www.hm-treasury.gov.uk/

It's your money. Here is where to get the latest reports, press releases and other information put forth by the Treasury on economic and financial matters.

This section provides information on sites where you can acquire e-commerce resources. It is organised according to the steps you might take to establish an e-business. Consult the section on internet marketing (page 12) first.

SITE BUILDER NETWORK (SBN) WORKSHOP

http://msdn.microsoft.com/workshop/default.asp

This site has everything that Microsoft wants you to know, use and above all buy from them to develop your site. Good source of information and tools, especially if you already use Microsoft products.

GROUP MAIL

http://www.group-mail.com/download.html

A utility to send e-mails to a list of people is an excellent way to market over the web. This product (like many others) manages the task easily.

MAILLOOP

http://www.mailloop.com/

Another excellent bulk mailing program, Mailloop can send automated personalised e-mails to targeted lists. There is a difference between this and hijacking your ISP's mail server to send 100,000 spam messages. The demo version of Mailloop has limited functionality but allows you a good evaluation.

MAIL KING

http://www.mailking.com/

Everyone dreads the 'Dear Customer' standard e-mail. One of the time-consuming tasks in automating and personalising your sales e-mail is importing your contact databases, spreadsheets and e-mail address books. Mail King can access them directly without the need to import and produce personalised, targeted e-mails.

Positioning

POSITION AGENT
http://www.positionagent.com/

Why is no one visiting your site? One reason may be that it does not score highly on search engines, even after you have tweaked your Meta tags (see Meta Medic, below). A position agent helps you to monitor and manipulate search engine rankings. You may or may not choose to pay the £40 per year or £10 per month fees, but there is a free trial – check out your own site's rankings on 12 major search engines.

META MEDIC
http://www.northernwebs.com/set/setsimjr.html#caveats

Once you have a commercial web site, you need to know that search engines can find and rank it. This is often a function of the Meta tags at the top of your web page. Getting these right is not the black art it is made out to be, but designing search engine friendly web pages does require some attention to Meta tag details. Meta Medic is a freeware web spider plus syntax checker. Enter your site's URL via this page and it will produce a report on your Meta tags. Extremely useful, fast and simple.

Site Promotion

VIEW FREE CLASSIFIED ADS ON VERYHOT.COM
http://www.veryhot.com/classifieds/viewads.html

VeryHOT.com is a busy site with classified adverts arranged by categories including Vendors, Money Making Opportunities, Financial, Business Opportunities, Travel, Import-Export, How To Books (no relation to the publisher of this book), Computer Products, Real Estate, Professional Services, Merchandising, Personal Products and Health & Beauty. They can also be searched by keywords. This is an easily navigated place to start and a good site to place your ad.

INTERNET NEWS BUREAU
http://www.newsbureau.com/

For a fee (about £150), INB will send a press release about your site to some 1,200 on-line services which like to know such things. This is also a good place to read on-line press releases. It is well categorised and easy to use.

12FREE   http://1-2-free.com/

There are any number of banner exchange programs. This is one which allows your site to earn credits and payments. It also explains the banner exchange system in more detail. If you would like to explore others there is a list at http://www.veryhot.com/hotprom.htm

1ST GLOBAL LINK DIRECTORY   http://www.123link.com/12free/

Likewise, link exchanges are a good web site promotional aid. This is one of the top 100 business directories which provides a free basic listing of your web site on the 1st Global Directory™ of Products & Services and membership of the link exchange programme.

HYPER BANNER SERVICES   http://www.hyperbanner.net/earn.dbm#ecom

For an all-in-one service, this is hard to beat. Apart from banner link exchanges, the site gives access to Cash-It (which puts links on your site to e-merchants, who will pay for traffic and sales and do the book-keeping); Hyper-Deal (an instant e-commerce presence); E-Commerce Tips (more facts about e-business) and more.

Transactions

ELECTRONIC TRANSFER.COM   http://www.electronictransfer.com/

Someone has to handle your credit card processing, merchant accounts and payment systems. Electronic Transfer.com are by no means the only ones, and this is not a recommendation. But their site is a useful source of information on this complex area of e-business, even if you don't decide to take their services.

And finally...

FIFEWEB CYBERMARKETING   http://www.fifeweb.net/cybermarketing

This site provides a one-stop resource for all aspects of e-business, including everything above and more. But, as the site author, I would say that, wouldn't I?

See also 'Free Stuff' (page 11).

FREE STUFF SUPERSITE   http://members.aol.com/drctmktgrp/page3.html

There are tools and 'dongles' that any web designer needs, especially if building an e-commerce or marketing site. This page has links to a number of these, including free autoresponders, links swap (try Best Links or Soprano), your own free classified ads site, information on how to build your own banner system (not free), help to Tune Up Your HTML, free site content (News, Market, Sports, Weather etc) and a free Fax On Demand Service. The quality is variable but the choice, eventually, is yours.

INSTANT PUBLISHER   http://www.eyelandenterprises.com/publisher.htm

One thing that bamboozles people wishing to set up an e-commerce site is – what on earth do I sell? One answer is information. But where to get it? One place to start is with free 'How To Do It' pamphlets which can be printed, downloaded from your site or e-mailed. This site is an order form for a CD-ROM with 750 information booklets, some of them useful for e-commerce web site builders themselves, such as The Mail Order Beginner's Business Guide, Get A VISA/MasterCard With No Credit, Starting An Import Business From Home, Write A Job Winning Resumé, Write Profitable Classified Ads and How To Write A Press Release. The focus is very American (How To Find Work With the Federal Government, for example) but the CD may be worth the £30 it will probably cost with shipping. Another source of similar content is http://premiumbiz.com/report2000.htm

101 FREE STUFF LINKS   http://www.sharewareplace.com/101/101free.shtml

This is another collection of links to various categories of free things, worth investigating.

MAKE MONEY ON-LINE!   http://yourmate.hypermart.net/index.html

Anyone looking for an on-line business opportunity should investigate this site, if only to see what other people are doing. There are also links to programs which will help establish an e-enterprise.

Anyone selling anything via the web needs a set of tools and some information on how to go about it. This section provides background information on this area, while the section on e-commerce (page 7) contains the resources required to establish an e-business. The section on shopping (page 80) also has information on aspects of electronic commerce, security and precautions.

Background information

NET USE
http://www.bgsu.edu/departments/tcom/users.html

Dr Bruce Klopfenstein of Bowling Green University produced this comprehensive page of links to web user research. It contains every sort of web traffic analysis, some of it historical and therefore out of date, but still useful when planning an assault on the wired world.

ICONOCAST MARKET INTELLIGENCE
http://www.iconocast.com/index.html

ICONOCAST is a good, user-friendly resource for facts, statistics, trends, gossip and rumours in web marketing. It is written by Michael Tchong, founder of CyberAtlas, one of the best known market research sites. Expect weekly e-mails.

DTI SECURE ELECTRONIC COMMERCE STATEMENT
http://www.dti.gov.uk/cii/ana27p.html

The DTI is the UK government department most concerned with on-line marketing, e-commerce and electronic shopping. The report is worth reading for more information.

Overall help

THE MINING CO SMALL BUSINESS INFORMATION
http://sbinformation.miningco.com/

Those excellent people at Mining Co have a definitive guide to internet marketing with all sorts of useful links and resources. Comprehensive and thorough, this is somewhere to start when gathering information and tools.

THE E-COMMERCE ADVISOR   http://sotkin.com/nl/

This web marketing e-zine contains easy to understand articles, tips, resource links, and more in a very clear, uncluttered site that is worth emulating.

CLUETRAIN   http://www.cluetrain.com/

This collection of almost 100 articles on internet marketing is very thorough and covers all aspects of the subject in considerable depth.

NETSCAPE NETCENTRE E-BUSINESS BASICS

http://home.netscape.com/netcenter/smallbusiness/index.html

Netcentre is an extremely comprehensive service all about e-businesses. If you don't mind the regular e-mails and plethora of cookies designed to keep you tied into Netscape, then it provides an excellent guide to the world of electronic commerce. Especially useful is the tutorial, '7 Simple Steps' (which are, for the record, Get Email; Build a Web Site; Attract Visitors; Track Your Visitors; Improve Your Site; Find New Customers; and Sell Online). A good introduction to the field.

Hints and tips

INTERNET MARKETING CENTER   http://www.marketingtips.com/

If you are looking for alternative ways and up-to-date or innovative ideas for marketing your product or service on the web, this is a truly excellent source of good information. There are articles, hints, tips, information for small businesses and links to other sites of interest on the web.

JB PUBLICATIONS   http://www.jb-publications.com/

This good-looking site offers self-help books, audio tapes, business tools, business opportunities and software for the budding entrepreneur who wants to start or enhance a web site business.

THE PROFIT CLINIC　　　　　　　　　http://www.profitclinic.com/

This subversive and well-designed site is a must for anyone who wants to know the insider secrets of small business web marketing techniques. It is genuinely one of the best small business resources available, although some of the features and special offers (free coaching, for instance) only work in Australia.

ART OF BUSINESS WEB SITE PROMOTION　　　http://www.deadlock.com/promote/

This is a good resource with excellent tutorials on site promotion, in-depth articles, on-line marketing strategies, links to software tools and resources. You do have to sign up for a free e-mail newsletter, but your e-mail address will not be passed on and you can unsubscribe any time.

QUALITY FREE ARTICLES　　　　　　　http://www.uni-sol.com/window/

Everything in this library of reports, articles and information for internet users is free to download. Tick the reports you want, enter your e-mail address and reports will be sent to you immediately. This requires, as you will have noticed, giving your e-mail address. There is an assurance that this will not be sold to mailing list holders or spammers and, to be fair, in a three-month period I received not one e-mail that could be traced back to this source. Much of the information is US-specific, but the rest has more general validity.

ART OF BUSINESS WEB SITE PROMOTION　　　http://www.deadlock.com/promote/

This is a very good resource. It has excellent in-depth tutorials on site promotion, comprehensive articles, clever on-line marketing strategies and links to resources and tools. You will have to sign up for the free newsletter (Deadlock Despatch), but e-mail addresses are not passed on and cancelling your subscription is easy.

A really good virus can ruin your whole day. This section lists a number of web sites which specialise in anti-virus information. Because the virus field moves so fast, and it is not always possible to find exactly what you need on any one site, a large number of alternatives is given. The first listing is of individuals or companies with anti-virus development expertise but not selling software or hardware as such.

CIAC (COMPUTER INCIDENT ADVISORY CAPABILITY)   http://ciac.llnl.gov/
COMPUTER SECURITY CENTER   http://www.csc.se/
HENRI DELGER'S VIRUS HELP AND INFORMATION
    http://pages.prodigy.com/virushelp/
KEN DUNHAM'S ANTI-VIRUS PAGE: http://antivirus.miningco.com/
EDINBURGH UNIVERSITY'S PC VIRUS PAGE
    http://mft.ucs.ed.ac.uk/pcvirus/pcvirus.htm
EICAR (EUROPEAN INSTITUTE FOR COMPUTER ANTI-VIRUS RESEARCH)
    http://www.eicar.com/
DAVID HARLEY'S PAGE   http://webworlds.co.uk/dharley/
HAVS (JOE HARTMANN'S ANTI-VIRUS SITE)   http://www.psnw.com/~joe/
DAVID HULL – COMPUTER VIRUSES AND SECURITY
    http://www.einet.net/galaxy/engineering/technology/computer-technology/
    security/david-hull/galaxy.htm
ICSA (INTERNATIONAL COMPUTER SECURITY ASSOCIATION)
    http://www.icsa.net/
INDIANAPOLIS UNIVERSITY COMPUTER VIRUS RESEARCH CENTRE
    http://www.indyweb.net/~cvhd/
MIKE LAMBERT'S VIRUS SITE   http://www.frontiernet.net/~mlambert/
MAILANDER'S DEN   http://www.agora.stm.it/htbin/wwx?fi^N.Ferri
DOUG MUTH'S HOMEPAGE   http://www.ezweb.net/dmuth/virus/index.html
NIST/CSL   http://csrc.ncsl.nist.gov/virus/
OPEN UNIVERSITY   http://www-tec.open.ac.uk/casg/avone.html
OXFORD UNIVERSITY COMPUTING SERVICES AV PAGE
    http://info.ox.ac.uk/OUCS/micros/virus/
PENN STATE ANTI-VIRUS PAGE   http://cac.psu.edu/~santoro/cac/virus.html
ROB ROSENBERGER'S 'COMPUTER VIRUS MYTHS' PAGE
    http://www.kumite.com/myths/
SANDRIN ANTI-VIRUS CONNECTION   http://members.home.net/sandrin/

SECURE COMPUTING MAGAZINE	http://www.westcoast.com/
SLOVAK ANTIVIRUS CENTRE	http://ftp.elf.stuba.sk/packages/pub/pc/
THOMAS JEFFERSON UNIVERSITY'S VIRUS INFORMATION PAGE	
	http://www.tju.edu/tju/dis/ic/virus/
THE VIRUS RESEARCH UNIT AT THE UNIVERSITY OF TAMPERE, FINLAND	
	http://www.uta.fi/laitokset/virus
THE VTC (VIRUS TEST CENTER) AT THE UNIVERSITY OF HAMBURG, GERMANY	
	http://agn-www.informatik.uni-hamburg.de/vtc/naveng.htm
MARK WEST'S ANTI-VIRUS SITE	http://www.hitchhikers.net/av.shtml
EDDY WILLEMS' ANTI-VIRUS SITE	http://www.club.innet.be/~ewillems/

The second listing is of companies who sell anti-virus products. This is rather over-complete, but many readers will have pre-installed anti-virus software and will wish to upgrade. If not, three good places to start are:

SYMANTEC ANTIVIRUS RESEARCH CENTER (NORTON ANTIVIRUS TOOLKIT)	
	http://www.symantec.com/region/reg_eu/avcenter/
DR SOLOMONS	http://www.drsolomon.com/
MCAFEE	http://www.mcafee.com/

Others (with software product names) are:

ALWIL SOFTWARE *AVAST!, AVAST32*	http://www.anet.cz/alwil/
ANYWARE SOFTWARE *ANYWARE ANTIVIRUS*	http://www.helpvirus.com/
AVP (ANTIVIRAL TOOLKIT PRO)	http://www.command-hq.com/command/
CALLUNA TECHNOLOGY *HARDWALL*	http://www.calluna.com
CAT COMPUTER SERVICES *QUICK HEAL*	http://www.quickheal.com
CHEKWARE *CHEKMATE, CHEKWORD*	http://chekware.simplenet.com/
CHEYENNE INOCULAN	http://www.cheyenne.com/security/
COMMAND SOFTWARE	http://www.commandcom.com/
CSIR VIRUS PROTECTION	http://www.vps.co.za/
CYBEC *VET ANTIVIRUS*	http://www.cybec.com.au/
CYBERSOFT *V-FIND*	http://www.cyber.com/
DATA FELLOWS *F-SECURE ANTI-VIRUS*	http://www.datafellows.com/
DIALOGUESCIENCE *DRWEB, ADINF*	http://www.dials.ru/
ELIASHIM/ESAFE	http://www.eliashim.com/
EMD ENTERPRISES *EMD ARMOR PLUS*	http://www.emdent.com/
ESET *NOD-ICE, NOD32*	http://www.eset.sk/
FOREFRONT *FOREFRONT ANTI-VIRUS*	http://www.ffg.com/products/pc/anti.html
FRISK SOFTWARE *F-PROT*	http://www.complex.is/

GECAD *ROMANIAN ANTIVIRUS (RAV)* — http://www.gecad.ro/
H+BEDV DATENTECHNIK *ANTIVIR* — http://www.antivir.de/
HIGHER GROUND DIAGNOSTICS *IMMUNE II* — http://www.uglyware.com/
HIWIRE COMPUTER & SECURITY *FRONTLINE* — http://www.hiwire.com.sg/
IBM *IBM ANTI-VIRUS* — http://www.av.ibm.com/
IKARUS VIRUS *UTILITIES* — http://www.ikarus.at/
INTEL *LANDESK VIRUS PROTECT* — http://www.intel.com/network/virus/
IRIS *ANTIVIRUS PLUS* — http://www.irisav.com/
KASPERSKY LABS *AVP (ANTIVIRAL TOOLKIT PRO)* — http://www.avp.ru/
LEPRECHAUN *VIRUS BUSTER* — http://www.leprechaun.com.au/
LOOK *VIRUS ALERT, VIRUS ALERT FOR MACROS* — http://www.look.com/
MICROWORLD *RED ARMOUR* — http://www.microworldsystems.com/products.html
MKS *MKS VIR* — http://www.mks.com.pl/
NETPRO *PC SCANMASTER, SERVER SCANMASTER* — http://www.netpro.com/
NETWORK ASSOCIATES *VIRUSSCAN, WEBSHIELD* — http://www.nai.com/
NETZ COMPUTING *INVIRCIBLE, RESQDISK, RESQDATA* — http://www.invircible.com/
NORMAN DATA DEFENSE SYSTEMS *NORMAN VIRUS CONTROL*

http://www.norman.no/english.htm
OVERBYTE CORPORATION *DISQUICK DISKETTES* — http://www.disquick.com/
PANDA SOFTWARE *PANDA ANTIVIRUS* — http://www.pandasoftware.com/
PARSONS TECHNOLOGY *VIRUCIDE PLUS* — http://www.parsonstech.com/utilities/
PER SYSTEMS *PER ANTIVIRUS* — http://www.persystems.com/antivir/
PORTCULLIS COMPUTER SECURITY *DEFUSE ENTERPRISE*

http://www.portcullis-security.com/
PROLAND SOFTWARE *PROTECTOR PLUS* — http://www.pspl.com/
QUARTERDECK CORPORATION *VIRUSWEEP* — http://www.quarterdeck.com/quarc/
REFLEX MAGNETICS *DISKNET* — http://www.reflex-magnetics.co.uk/
RG SOFTWARE SYSTEMS *VI-SPY, NO MORE #*!$ VIRUSES*

http://www.rg-av.com/
SAFETYNET *VIRUSNET-PRO* — http://www.safe.net/
SBABR *SYSTEM BOOT AREAS ANTIVIRUS* — http://www.sbabr.com/
SECURENET TECHNOLOGIES *V-NET, MACRO-BLASTER, MACRO-BLASTER 97*

http://www.securenet.org/
SOPHOS *DFENCE, ANTIVIRUS* — http://www.sophos.com/
STILLER RESEARCH *INTEGRITY MASTER* — http://www.stiller.com/
SYBARI SOFTWARE *GROUPWARE ANTI-VIRUS SOLUTIONS FOR NOTES AND EXCHANGE*

http://www.sybari.com/
TREND MICRO *PC-CILLIN, INTERSCAN VIRUSWALL* — http://www.antivirus.com/
VDS *VDS, PERFORIN FOR WINWORD* — http://www.vdsarg.com/

Finding graphics is one of the main reasons people surf the web – whether it's a picture for a document, clipart for a report or an animation for a web site, there is no doubt that each one is worth a thousand words, at least in terms of download time.

Animated gifs

There is nothing quite like an animated gif to liven up your web page. These are moving images constructed like one of those flip-book cartoons – each image, a gif file in its own right, is slightly different from the one before and they are displayed in a sequence to give the impression of movement. The number of 'frames', the speed (frames per second), whether it is transparent (the background shows through) or opaque, and whether the animation displays once or loops indefinitely (in fact, usually about 1,000 times after each page load) can usually be controlled when the gifs are created. You may wish to create your own gifs, in which case there are excellent programs like **anim.exe** which comes with **Paint Shop Pro 5.0** or Microsoft's own **Gif Animator.** On the other hand, there are many galleries of animated gifs on the web, some of which you can use freely and some of which require either an acknowledgement or some form of payment. There is nothing to stop anyone downloading an animated gif from a web page (see below) except that it's illegal to use it if it's copyright, unless the owner gives permission. But it can be worth downloading interesting animations to see how they work, frame by frame. Do not redistribute any graphics in on-line galleries, CD-ROMs or other methods unless you have express permission.

Another legality to watch – it is often said that the web is unregulated, but put a moving image in your site and you may be considered a 'broadcaster', just like a TV station.

Downloading an image

Right-click (PC) or click and hold (Mac), then select 'Save Image As...' (Netscape) or 'Save Picture As...' (Internet Explorer). You can choose to change the name if you wish – it may, for instance, be called the same as an image you already have. Save the image in the folder where you keep your own web page files. Edit your web page and place the image where you like. Some web page editors such as FrontPage allow drag and drop placement. If you are editing the HTML directly using Notepad or another text editor, use the <img> tag: <img src="pic.gif"> where pic.gif is the name of the image you saved. Check that your HTML is correct by viewing the page in your browser. If you see the image appear on your page correctly, then upload the image and the amended web page to your web server. This is covered in more detail in *Creating a Web Site* by Bruce Durie, from How To Books.

NETSCAPE BACKGROUNDS   http://www.netscape.com/assist/net_sites/bg/backgrounds.html

Use Netscape's backgrounds, either by downloading them or by referring to the Netscape server (in which case they may load quickly). A good collection on a very simple page.

ALLI'S BACKGROUNDS   http://www.tecinfo.com/~alli/ani/bkgrnd.htm

Tiling backgrounds, textures, desktop wallpaper and everything you need are collected and categorised on this nice, simple site. Lovely muzak in the background, too.

CRAMES STUDIO   http://www.weare3d.com/asite/download.html

All of the images in this collection of 3-D animated gifs are free to use but they do ask you to link to Crames Studios. Otherwise contact them for licensing information. The site contains detailed instructions and tips on saving and installing animations and how to link to Crames.

SHARDS OF LIGHT   http://davis.wpi.edu/~spanky/artlight.html

Some gif sites consist of pages heavily loaded with graphics and pages of animations which are therefore slow to load. This is one. However, the artwork in Shards of Light is stunning. John Stevens' artworks are created in Pov Ray and Bryce 2, as well as some others in more traditional media. This link is to the less graphically intense pages. Others are, as the author himself says, 'browser cracking'. Good links to 3-D art resources such as the Pov Ray raytracing program.

XARA ANIMATED GIF COMPETITION RESULTS
http://www.xara.com/noframes/corelxara/contest.html

CorelXARA is a useful program for image creation, and Corel recently ran an animated gif competition judged by the staff of Xara Ltd. This site has some interesting and imaginative animations, not all created using XARA.

SCUBAMOM'S ICONS & ANIMATIONS
http://www.scubamom.com/animations/

ScubaMom is clearly an interesting person, if somewhat fish-fixated. If you like fish, you'll love this site of animated gifs on fishy themes.

KARMASTORM GALLERY
http://www.tfs.net/~stevenb/ksgall01.htm

Steve Bennett's awesome web site has some of the most stunning animated images available anywhere, many with Steve's own comments. There are images of trains, fantasy themes (birds, dragons etc), small rotating stars and skies. Check out the Ares.gif and The Fish in OuterSpace. The site also contains images from other artists.

AGL LIBRARY
http://www.arosnet.se/agl/library/libraryindexhome.html

The Animated Gif Library (AGL) is a site dedicated to all aspects of gif animation, with a searchable database of images, tips, links and other useful information. AGL says all images on the site are free and legal to use, but do check with the originators. This site also includes chat, free electronic postcards, good links to other sites with free services and an animated gif search engine which provides links to other animated gif collections. A good place to start.

WEBPEDIA GIFS
http://www.webpedia.com/animations/animations/

This sub-site claims to be one of the largest animated gif collections on the web and also has a great deal of information about creating animations. It is organised alphabetically and some gifs are themed (Easter, Christmas etc).

ELATED ANIMATED BUTTONKIT   http://www.elated.com/toolbox/buttonkits/

Elated are well known for web design and for offering free
web page templates. Here, they also offer a collection of gif
images, free to use if you put a link to the Elated Web Toolbox
on your site. This is an increasingly common form of free
advertising, but why not? One of the growing uses for
animated gifs is in animated 'rollover' buttons which change
when clicked or passed over with the mouse. This site has link
instructions and 20 different 'button kits' containing 800 or so
buttons, organised by logical headings. Helpfully, the images
are colour-coded as suitable for white, black or any
backgrounds. It also includes something I've always wanted –
don't ask me why – a gif of every key on the PC keyboard!

PIONEER HALL   http://members.aol.com/royalef1/pioneer.htm

This collection of gif links (some out of date and not working)
is remarkable for being the first such site and includes some of
the very first pages ever to use the 89a interlaced gif format. It
is completely 'undesigned' but has historical interest
nonetheless and is a good place to start link-chasing. See the
related EXPO site below.

THE EXPO   http://members.aol.com/royalef1/expo.htm

See Pioneer Hall (above). A nice touch is a preview window
(using frames).

MICROMOVIE MINIMULTIPLEX   http://www.teleport.com/~cooler/mmmm/

Nicely organised into themed areas, this site uses a 'movie
theatre' analogy to help navigate the collection of gifs. Good
use of frames, such as a preview window.

2COOL ANIMATIONS   http://www.gifanimations.com/

A well-categorised site with around 900 animated gifs to
download and use on your web pages. Set up with frames and
20 categories.

ANIMATED WINDOWS ICONS — http://www.akula.com/~hovey/icons.htm

These are not animated gifs, but icon files. If you have ever wished you could change your Windows icons and cursors and get rid of the default hourglass and program pointers, this is the site. It holds a collection of 100 icons and cursors for the Windows 95 or 98 desktop, in a downloadable 375KB zip file which expands into PC compatible .ico or .ani format.

ALEX'S ANIMATED GIF SHOP — http://www.wsdaents.com/

This is the granddaddy of them all – over 2,500 animated gifs, many in a pay area ($30) but some in a free area mainly themed as Animals, Baby, Transport and Xmas.

ANIMATION FACTORY — http://www.animfactory.com/

Free animated gifs, clipart and graphics.

CLIPART CASTLE — http://www.clipartcastle.com/jokers/animatedgifs.htm

Anyone who needs fantasy-themed gifs for Dungeons and Dragons sites and so on will find just about everything they need here. A nice touch is the castle theme on the site itself, which will make it attractive to Doom gamers and fantasy fans.

ART TODAY — http://www.arttoday.com/PD-0025000/

Art Today is one of the best-designed sites in this category, as you might expect, but rarely get, from an on-line art site. It has good quality clipart, buttons, arrows, bullets, graphics, backgrounds, rules, textures, icons, photos and animated gifs. This site offers 40,000 images free if you subscribe (free) and 250,000 if you pay an annual subscription of around £20. The free subscription is worth it if you don't mind being pestered by e-mails urging you to pay up and get the full collection. Unsubscribing to the e-mail messages removes access to the free service.

BARRY'S CLIP ART — http://www.barrysclipart.com/

Among the images by various (credited) web image artists

there are 400 useful animations. Many of these images were apparently collected from sites while surfing the net. This may mean that some are copyright.

PHOENIX GIF COLLECTION   http://www.ala-net.com/phoenix/animated.html

This is a gorgeously simple site. Phoenix has understood the fact that putting multiple animated gifs on one web page can place heavy demands on some PCs, take an age to load and sometimes destabilise the browser. Therefore, the page is a simple list of clickable links with a brief description for each one.

This section could go on for ever. Anyone into computer games tends to be into the web as well, although the reverse is not necessarily true. Therefore, the links below are a combination of sites from which to get games, sites about games and sites for gamers. Enjoy!

FILE LIBRARY AT CHANNEL 1: GAMES

http://www.filelibrary.com/contents/windows/115/27.html

This site features fast downloads and easy navigation to 125,000 virus-checked files but, cleverly, requires registration to get a download quota, after which you have to buy more 'allowance'. This also lets them have your e-mail address which, although kept confidential, will be used to inform you of 'offers'. However, it's a large, useful and robust site with few pretensions.

SHAREWARE.COM

http://www.shareware.com/

Clicking on Games in this huge site takes you to the sister site download.com. This is absolutely the place to get your Virtual Bridge or the latest bug fixes for Soulblighter. It is excellent for downloading demos, and helpfully tells you the file size so that you know the Ace Ventura Demo weighs in at 23.9MB before you download it (as 304,478 others have, apparently).

HAPPY PUPPY

http://www.happypuppy.com/compgames/index.html

Sorry, I just like the title. However, it does have the latest PC, Mac and console games, web games (on-line, multiplayer) plus hints and cheats. Even if the cute canine motif wears thin after a while, the navigation is excellent and the search facility fast. Intriguing contests are offered.

GAMESPOT

http://www.gamespot.com/

This is a truly comprehensive site for game fanatics. Good for downloads of demos, it also has news, reviews, previews, hints, features, designer diaries, columns, letters, a beta-test version centre, contests and a release calendar. Nicely designed and fast loading, a particularly good feature is the 3-D model gallery, in which are the tools to grab a character, creature or weapon from your favorite game and manipulate it.

VIRTUAL GAMEBOY http://www.komkon.org/fms/vgb/vgbwindows.html

It might seem a bit second-hand, but there is a way to play GameBoy games on your PC with this software.

GAMES DOMAIN http://www.gamesdomain.com/

The original web game site has undergone a radical redesign but offers the classic combination of large database, easy searches and fairly fast downloads

---

WINSITE http://www.winsite.com/

This is an immense shareware collection with very easy search capabilities.

JUMBO http://www.jumbo.com/

Another huge (over 300,000) collection of shareware and freeware programs, albeit slow to load.

WIREPLAY http://www.wireplay.com/

If anyone is going to get rich from on-line games networks, it's the phone companies. BT therefore set up Wireplay, organised into 'clans' called The Badgers of Oblivion, the Justified Ancients of Menace and the like. Games range from puzzles to arcade-style shoot-ups, and the most popular of all is Quake.

THRUSTWORLD http://www.thrustworld.co.uk

One of the first ever games networks, Thrustworld has continued to improve and boasts dazzling speed for even the most complex graphics.

BEZERK http://www.bezerk.com/

If you haven't played You Don't Know Jack, you're no web-head.

INTERNET GAMING ZONE
http://www.zone.com/

This zone has free membership, unlike some.

GAME REVOLUTION MAGAZINE ONLINE
http://www.game-revolution.com/

This is an excellent source of reviews of games for PC, Mac, Saturn, Playstation, Nintendo 64 and Dreamcast and despite being graphics-laden, loads quickly. Gamers will always find something new here. The Red Alert Strategy Document has become the constant reading of one very happy seven-year-old would-be world conqueror.

NETGAMER
http://www.netgamer.net/

This on-line magazine is the best-known forum for information on developments in the world of games.

SEGA
http://www.sega.com/

This site is notable for its remarkably minimalist design. It has lots for the dedicated Sega PC gamer, including downloads, patches and news of upcoming releases.

It may seem perverse to have a book aimed at PC users discussing games available on a completely different system, but I am assured by my seven-year-old consultant that 'everybody' has both. In any case, there is no connection to the web from PSX (although I have no idea why not, given the advances in TV-based internet) and there are many excellent resources for gamers on the Web. ○ △ □ ⊗ as they say.

PLAYSTATION CHEAT.NET http://www.internet.de/~cwirth/gcheats.html

Just what it says, this is an outstanding if no frills informational site with game FAQs, walkthroughs, tips and a page of 'cheats' and passwords for about 1,200 games! If it really has had nearly a million hits, as the counter claims, it deserves them. Hardware is also dealt with. Walkthrough, as the name implies, is a complete solution to a game. A really clever use of an image map gives site navigation to an image of a Playstation console. An alphabetical anchor tag list would help navigate, as in PlayStation Gamer (see below).

PLAYSTATION GAMER – CHEATS http://www.sol.no/games/psgamer/cheats.htm

Alphabetical navigation and search by name put this site onto the map. Although it is nowhere near as complete as Playstation cheat.net (above) it does boast over 400 entries.

PLAYSTATION AND N64 http://www1.stuttgart.netsurf.de/~schmied/home.htm

This site has neat use of animated gifs and navigation to pages of Playstation, N64 and other games, marred only by the annoying use of Quicktime plug-ins which take an age to load (at my connection speed). This is a German site which recognises the pre-eminence of English and has pages and links in both languages.

WELCOME TO PSX NATION http://www.psxnation.com/

One for the real hard-core fans here, it is well-presented, easily navigable and not too slow-footed. Paradise for the converted.

MINING CO. VIDEO GAMES   http://videogames.miningco.com/

The good people at The Mining Co (see page 91) can be relied upon to put together a good listing, and this one is no exception.

You can spend hours in search engines finding the best software for a particular job. Or you may not even know that a particular piece of software exists, or even that you need it. Software archives with links to downloads are the answer.

SOFTSEEK   http://www.softseek.com

This may well be the best place to check out and download the latest software. It has a dated look, but is well organised into a hierarchy of meaningful categories. Features include New Releases, Top Downloads, Editors' Picks and a good search engine. A minor gripe is that it doesn't show file sizes in the descriptions generated by searches, so it's not immediately obvious whether it's worth looking at the description of a 40MB file you're never going to download. It does say whether the download is shareware, freeware, a timed trial or a demo. Newsletter sign-up available. Links to providers' home pages.

DAVE CENTRAL   http://www.davecentral.com/

Quirky, idiosyncratic and clearly one man's labour of love, Dave will keep you up to date on the latest shareware and freeware software for downloading. An interesting recent addition is a What's New ticker-tape – a small Java applet which displays everything added to the database that day. Dave also has domain name registration, a newsletter and links to providers' home pages.

FILEFARM   http://www.filefarm.com/

FileFarm is a well-organised and fully searchable site. The downloadable software is listed with descriptions, specifics, Latest Update, Top Downloads and not too much extraneous advertising. You can also sign up for the weekly newsletter covering new and upcoming files. No Macintosh or UNIX support – coming soon, apparently. Links to providers' home pages.

TUCOWS   http://www.tucows.com/

The rather unusual acronym for this site means The Ultimate
Collection of Winsock Software. The site has expanded from
just Winsock utilities since it was launched in 1992, but the
name – and the obvious but appealing two cows logo – have
stayed. The farmyard theme continues with Head of the Herd
(editor's choice software, with the best getting five cows) and
eBarn (electronically Buy and register now) Store Best to
purchase software. Features include Editorial, Top Picks, a
good index, newsletter, pressroom, search, spotlight, CD-ROM
info and information on how to become an affiliate. The best
feature is the wide availability of mirror sites in Africa,
Australia, Canada, Caribbean, Central America/Mexico,
Europe, South America and the USA. Despite what anyone
says, geography does matter on the internet and the closer a
server is to you, the faster your downloads. The main
categories of software are Win 95/98 (mainly browsers, chat
and e-mail) Win NT, Win 3.x, Java, Mac, BeOS, Linux,
Gaming and PDA. There are links to providers' home pages.

GUERNSEY SHAREWARE LIBRARY   http://www.guernsey.net/software.html

This is a great example of a local service. If you happen to live
in the Guernsey.Net area you will be able to download
software from local servers and therefore quickly. The rest of
us get normal service. It also shows what can be done on
minimal resources, very simply. Few games, but worth a look
out of interest.

DOWNLOAD.COM   http://www.download.com

One of the biggest of the sites, Download offers the usual
collection of freeware, shareware and commercial software.

COMPLETELY FREE SOFTWARE   http://www.completelyfreesoftware.com/

Just what it says, CFS is nicely organised with a good index, a
New Software section, excellent search facilities and a special
section for web authors. A great feature is a £10 (roughly)
CD-ROM of software shipped free anywhere in the world.

FILEZ

http://www.filez.com

Filez looks good (apart from the irritating tendency, adopted from the hacking fraternity, of ending all plurals with a 'z') and loads fast with a claimed 75 million files to search! It also has useful Top 20 and What's New listings, plus the offer of a CD software collection.

BROWSER PLUG-INS

http://home.netscape.com/plugins/index.html

Plug-ins are small programs which help your browser play audio, video and other files. Netscape's official plug-in site is the best place to find plug-ins for Navigator/Communicator and also ActiveX controls, which perform the same function within Internet Explorer.

ELATED PAGEKITS

http://www.elated.com/toolbox/pagekits/

A great help to web designers, Elated page kits are sets of templates. These free starter packs are entire web-site templates, with code and images. Please mention and link to Elated if you use any of the buttons or one of the 15 different pagekits. They download in zip format.

MACROMEDIA WEB PLAYER DOWNLOAD CENTER

http://www.macromedia.com/shockwave/download/

This is the best place to get Shockwave and Flash programs. That's it.

WINPLANET – FRONT DOOR

http://www.winplanet.com/?filefarm.com

What is elegant about this site is that it combines download with news and reviews. A good way to keep up to date on software, hardware and related issues.

LINKOPEDIA FREEWARE

http://www.linkopedia.com/freeware.html

This is a simple list of links to freeware resources with a brief review. Very straightforward.

CONNECTFREE SOFTWARE   http://www.connectfree.co.uk/free_software/free_software.html

By way of contrast to Linkopaedia (above), here is a graphical version of the same idea. This free dial-up provider has usefully assembled about 20 free software sites on a single page with clickable buttons.

The Virtual Reality Modelling Language (VRML) is a standard language for describing interactive 3-D objects and worlds delivered across the internet. There are stunning walk-arounds and animations available, although they require a fast link, a high-spec PC and a tolerance of large phone bills. Viewing VRML worlds will usually require a plug-in or ActiveX component, but these are typically included with Version 4 of Netscape or Internet Explorer, or can be readily downloaded and installed. The Netscape Plug-ins page (http://home.netscape.com/plugins/) has Live 3D, Netscape's own VRML viewer, SGI's Cosmo Player and many other downloads.

THE VRML REPOSITORY   http://www.web3d.org/vrml/vrml.htm

The VRML Repository is an impartial and comprehensive source of information, tutorials, models, textures, links and recommended readings on VRML. Maintained by the Web3D Consortium as a public resource, this is the best site to start for VRML tools, tips and links, especially for those new to the idea of 3-D web browsing.

SILICON GRAPHICS   http://www.sgi.com/virtual_reality/

SGI has done more for VRML and virtual reality than almost anyone else, and deserves a mention. This page has many links and tutorials for VRML. Some of these require SGI's Cosmo Player to view the worlds.

MDL-CHIME   http://www.mdli.co.uk/

One of the best uses for VRML is the rendition of 3-D molecules. Elsevier's site is a good place to download Chime, a Netscape plug-in for chemical structure representation from polymers and proteins to chemical reactions. There are also links to good Chime sites, such as Brookhaven National Laboratory's Protein Data Bank, one of the world's foremost sources of protein structure information.

GRAFMAN http://www.graphcomp.com/vrml/pics.html

This gallery requires the Silicon Graphics Cosmo Player (see page 33)and has a good collection of VRML worlds, avatars and objects, with tutorials and notes on how they were created.

VRML CITY http://www.geocities.com/heartland/park/2818/index.html

This site is a small but very interesting use of embedding VRML worlds.

NANOHOME http://www.nanohome.com/nanohome/middle/middle3.html

Tired of flat web pages? NanoHome offers a 3-D version of your home page. This is actually a very clever advertising/ marketing idea dressed up as a service, but it has its place. NanoHome gives you a virtual reality web site (on the NanoHome server) and allows you to populate it with your favourite web links and fill it with interesting objects such as furniture and art. The registration process asks for a disturbing amount of personal information but if you are comfortable with this, build a home and reserve the sites 'next door' for your friends. Have a look at Jim Morrison's (The Doors) to see what is on offer. You will have to allow the viewer to download onto your PC.

CYBERTOWN http://www.cybertown.com/live3d/vrml20/space/space.html

Get on board a space ship and explore it, then check out the other parts of Cybertown. This evolving project is a nice use of VRML to create different sorts of visual effects and experiences.

MARS EXPLORATION http://mpfwww.jpl.nasa.gov/

NASA's Jet Propulsion Lab (JPL) has chronicled its Microrover landing on Mars, which provided a wealth of information about Mars. Using VRML, anyone can explore the Mars surface from this web site. See also http://www.bchip.com/mars/nav.html

ZACH'S VRML WORLD http://arapaho.nsuok.edu/~nsuhoa12/

This is a good implementation of VRML that strays into the world of interactive gaming. 'Be warned, this world is guarded by strict images who punish any infraction with a firey death!' it says. Have a walk around.

VRML VOYAGER http://members.tripod.com/~acerlord/vrml.htm#voyager

This 3-D view of Star Trek's lost ship is, like much VRML, very slow to load. But if you have the patience it is well worth an exploration. Other examples of VRML worlds are good, too – Pirates is interesting.

COOL VRML SITES http://www.3d-design.com/vrmlsite.html

This is an excellent, if undocumented source of links to other VRML sites.

See also the Natural History Museum link in the Museums section (pages 139 and 142).

One of the main demands on the web is for pictures of famous buildings. One reason may be the wholly natural desire to see places and structures that you may never go to for real or cannot find in standard coffee-table books. Then again, it may be no more than a need to see interesting pictures. Beyond that, architects are among the more graphically and technically aware communities and are therefore naturally in the forefront of web-enablement. This section deals with both the 'picture postcard' needs of the general public and the more specific professional requirements of architects themselves. Either way, enjoy, but beware of downloading something that belongs (at least in terms of the images) to someone else.

ARCHITECTURE ONLINE http://web.mit.edu/museum/exhibits/online.html

MIT's virtual gallery of architecture contains the collection of William Robert Ware who set up America's first formal architectural course. Ware began an intensive study of European courses and from this designed the first American architectural curriculum. This site also links to the other MIT Museum pages, all worth a look in their own right.

ARTSERVE http://rubens.anu.edu.au/

Want to see all the great buildings of Europe? Trust the Australians to help. The Australian National University (ANU) Art History & Visual Studies department has amassed 80,000 images on Art and Architecture, mainly from the Mediterranean, most unavailable elsewhere on the web. There is a good search engine for the whole site. Small images can be downloaded free of charge. Higher resolution images can be seen, but first register, pay and use the secure server. The Architecture index (https://rubens.anu.edu.au/architectureindex.html) is excellently structured and linked and takes you to all the famous buildings you only ever see on postcards. Also included are sub-sites on Canberra, Classical, Rome (post-classical), Student Projects, typefaces, icons, books and so forth.

AEC INFOCENTER http://www.aecinfo.com/

Called 'The Internet Expo for architecture, engineering and construction', this a good resource site for professionals. It includes access to software for CAD, design, photogrammetry, contracts management and geographic imaging. This is a good example of how a commercial company can profit from providing accessible information easily. It also has good forums (Construction Law, Green Building etc), though very US-oriented.

FACILITIES NET http://www.facilitiesnet.com/index.shtml

Another site for building construction, design and management professionals, this site is a source of information on issues that concern them. The site allows a search of the leading magazines in the industry and forums to exchange information with others. For anyone wishing to practise in North America, the job postings and salary database, news and regulatory reports will be useful. Otherwise, it's a good browse.

FRANK LLOYD WRIGHT SOURCE PAGE http://www.cypgrp.com/flw/

This huge resource site has more than 700 links with a chronological list of all the structures designed by Wright that were built and a Tourist path which lists all public structures and those which offer tours. The Links page is well categorised.

SUSTAINABLE ARCHITECTURE

http://members.aol.com/reidybrown/htmldocs/architecture/archpg1.html

This amateur site calls itself 'A guide to finding out more than you ever wanted to know' and is a good example of how the web can be used by individuals, then the results made widely available. The author, Reidy Brown, could not find any comprehensive information source on sustainable or passive solar architecture. So he wrote to students, teachers and professionals in the field to ask which graduate schools had a good reputation in environmentally conscious architecture. The results are here, with a plethora of good links.

Rather than listing individual charities, this section deals with resources for charity fundraisers and the relatively new field of internet fundraising.

FUNDERFINDER   http://www.funderfinder.org.uk/links.html

This organisation sells fundraising management software, but the site also has a good set of valuable links, including advice and guidance.

UK FUNDRAISING   http://www.fundraising.co.uk/

A good resource for UK charity and non-profit organisation fundraisers, this web site has a great deal of practical advice and access to expertise, particularly on fundraising using the internet and web. There are good examples of on-line fundraising.

ANGELS   http://www.angels.org.uk/

This is a free charity Internet Service Provider. Charities hosting their sites here get free local call rate dial-up internet access, 50MB web space, up to five e-mail addresses, Press Association news, local event details and the Lycos and Scoot search engines. They also get a percentage of visitors' telephone charges to their sites. Blue Cross, the Multiple Sclerosis Society, Arthritis Research Campaign and Great Ormond Street Hospital already use the service.

YAHOO! AUCTION SITE   http://auctions.yahoo.co.uk/

Yahoo! hosts charity auctions on-line at a UK site. These are increasingly popular as fundraising activities, so there is a queue.

THE ARTS COUNCIL   http://www.artscouncil.org.uk

Some arts organisations are charities, and will find the Arts Council of England's introduction to the UK arts funding system useful.

CHARITIES AID FOUNDATION   http://www.charitynet.org/caf/grants/index.html

CAF is a grant-awarding body – it disburses £400,000 each year of its own, and more on behalf of government, companies, trusts, foundations and other donors. But it is also an information resource for charities and donors. Experts help charities increase efficiency, develop new initiatives and find grants.

CHARITYNET   http://www.charitynet.org/

This is a good general resource, providing information, resources, tools and guidance of relevance to charities all over the world.

There is an enormous amount of environmental information on the web, much of it from groups of enthusiasts (and sometimes outright cranks) who have spotted the potential of essentially free propaganda distribution.

THE GREEN CHANNEL HOME PAGE http://www.greenchannel.com/

TGC gets more than 5 million visits a year – and it's not hard to see why. This is an extremely comprehensive site for news and views and information on campaigns, initiatives and events aimed at promoting positive environmental change by better communication of environmental information.

SITES OF ECOLOGICAL INTEREST http://eagle.bio.unipr.it/ecowww.html

---

This is merely a large list of links to other sites, but is a reasonable starting point for deeper research.

VIRTUAL LIBRARY OF ECOLOGY AND BIODIVERSITY http://conbio.rice.edu/vl/

The Center for Conservation Biology Network at Rice University maintains an excellent site dedicated to information on global sustainability, endangered species and much more. Easily browsable or searchable, it also has a superbly detailed History of Life section, albeit very textual rather than image-filled.

K-12:ECOLOGY/ENVIRONMENT http://www.ceismc.gatech.edu/busyt/eco.html

---

Georgia Institute of Technology maintains an extensive set of educational links about ecology and the environment, and contributes to the Globe project (see below).

THE GLOBE http://www.globe.gov/

Global Learning and Observations to Benefit the Environment (GLOBE) is a world-wide network of pupils and teachers from over 6,500 schools in more than 80 countries, working together with scientists to study the global environment. GLOBE students make environmental observations at or near their schools and report their data via the web. Scientists use this data in their research and provide feedback. The Global images based on student-collected data are available on the web.

AIR QUALITY INFORMATION FROM AUTOMATIC NETWORKS

http://www.aeat.co.uk/products/centres/netcen/aqarchive/scotsite.html

Smog in Sheffield or pollution in Peterborough – check here to see up-to-date information from automatic collection devices.

EPA FOR STUDENTS AND TEACHERS

http://www.epa.gov/epahome/students.htm

The US Environmental Protection Agency's web site has a wide and valuable collection of fact-sheets, interactive games and other resources to help schools study and understand the environment. Although aimed at the American schools curriculum, there is a lot for UK teachers and pupils too. Particularly good is 'Turning the Tide on Trash', a marine debris study guide with case studies.

FRIENDS OF THE EARTH SCOTLAND

http://www.foe-scotland.org.uk/

Environmental activists start here – although the site is slow to load (easy to fix, FOE!) it is packed with information on campaigns, briefing documents and extensive links to like-minded bodies. Particularly good are the sections on Get Your Beach Protected, the information on sustainable use of resources in Europe and schools projects.

WWF IN THE AMAZON

http://www.worldwildlife.org/

A single expanse of green covering more than two million square miles, the Amazon River basin is the world's richest rain forest with endangered species such as giant otters, manatees and harpy eagles, plus those intriguing coloured poison arrow frogs and the only nocturnal monkey. The Amazon basin has the greatest biological diversity on Earth – more than one-third of all the species in the world live there. Sights and Sounds of the Amazon is a great place to hear a macaw screech, a howler monkey howl or a jaguar roar.

Governments fall into two categories – those who want their citizens to have as much information as possible and those who want to restrict knowledge to the select few. Strangely, they come together on the web – even secretive governments with no open disclosure legislation (such as the UK) have remarkably complete informational sites, if you know where to look. And sometimes even paranoid governments share information with other countries which then publish it freely. Almost anything you want to know is published somewhere, although you may have to bounce off another nation to find it. Start here! On a more mundane level, what is your local council up to? And do they choose to tell you about it? Find out. The time of e-democracy is at hand.

OPEN GOVERNMENT	http://www.open.gov.uk/

The title says it all. The UK government is to be congratulated for putting so much out in the open in one place and making it so accessible. This is in marked contrast to the bad old days when government information meant worthy but dull films about making forks in Sheffield and how pickled walnuts were good for you. The best part of this site is the ready access to government departments' own sites and the area dedicated to the workings of Parliament. Teledemocracy is with us, albeit in a censored form. But see the White House site (below) for another way of doing things.

THE BRITISH MONARCHY	http://www.royal.gov.uk/

Affectionately known as 'One's Web site', this is testament to the Royal Family's stated aim of being closer and more accessible to the public. Monarchy Through The Ages is an excellent historical source for children, teachers and scholars and the virtual tour round the palaces and collections would put many museum web sites to shame. The design is suitably official, like an old passport and there are enough up-to-date pictures, stories and insider pieces to keep any Royals watcher happy for days. Nice one, Ma'am, and cheaper than a real visit to Buckingham Palace.

EUROPA HOMEPAGE   http://europa.eu.int/

This is the main front door to the European Union's Europa server and it's well worth it. Anything you would ever want to know about Europe and its institutions is there – and in 12 languages. It is far too huge to go into detail here, but it is easily searchable and stunningly well linked to other important information sources. If anything is worth the Euro budget, this site is it.

WELCOME TO THE WHITE HOUSE   http://www.whitehouse.gov/

Go talk to Bill. I did, and he – or his autobot, it's hard to tell the difference – replied within an hour. Any site which opens with 'The President and Vice President: their accomplishments, their families, and how to send them electronic mail' is just asking for it. Seriously, there is a stunning amount of information here, not just about America but also via the linked access to GovBot which can find over 1 million official US Government web pages and databases. Goodness knows how many UK laws I broke retrieving American documents on Britain's MI6, but they're all there, in the public domain.

LIBRARY OF CONGRESS   http://lcweb.loc.gov/homepage/lchp.html

This site could have appeared in any number of sections from Art to Reference to Science. This is America's memory and it contains important historical collections as well as a catalogue of text and images from major exhibitions, the THOMAS database of current and historical information on Congress, a Learning Page for students and teachers, plus digitised documents, films, photographs and sound recordings. By 2000 (the Library's bicentennial year) a collaboration with other major institutions will have digitised millions more items.

FEDERAL BUREAU OF INVESTIGATION   http://www.fbi.gov/

Who wouldn't want to see this? Would-be Elliot Nesses and Dana Scullys can check out the Special Agent eligibility criteria and fill in the on-line application form. An excellent feature from the renowned Forensic Laboratory is the retelling of famous investigations from the Lindbergh kidnapping to the World Trade Centre bombing. Not a mention of Monica Lewinsky's dress. Two really cute features are the FBI Tip Line – shop your neighbours – and the Kids and Teens sub-site, which has excellent educational material on Forensic Science, DNA Testing, Polygraph Testing, Fingerprinting and Internet Safety Tips for Kids. To become a Junior Special Agent, look at http://www.fbi.gov/kids/jsa/jsa.htm. If it lacks anything, it is the extra sparkle that the CIA site (http://www.odci.gov/cia/, see page 62) contains. As Tommy Lee Jones says in the famous quote from *Men In Black*: 'We're the FBI, Ma'am, we have no sense of humour that we are aware of'.

METROPOLITAN POLICE	http://www.met.police.uk/

It would be nice to be able to say that the New Scotland Yard web site knocks the FBI site into a pointed helmet, and, gratifyingly, it's the case! The design is gorgeous, the Recovered Property section an absolute hoot (the brave person who turns up to ask for the Bladed Weapons will be guaranteed Her Majesty's hospitality at one of the Windsor Group hotels) and the History sections are excellent. Sadly, some of the Java doesn't work, but that may be temporary. The Youth Pages have a neatly paradoxical feature which allows downloading of sounds but also discourages turning up the stereo on party nights. Overall, a nice bit of e-community policing, officer.

INTERPOL	http://www.interpol.com/

Not to be outdone, the world's intelligence service is also out to show its cuddly side and stop everyone thinking it is a secret police force. The very idea. The best feature is the Top 10 Most Wanted list. Anybody you know?

INTERNAL REVENUE SERVICE	http://www.irs.ustreas.gov/prod/

This makes our own Inland Revenue site – which is really all about how to fill in your tax forms – look like a well-meaning, cheerful but slightly staid uncle. The American IRS site is in the form of a local newspaper with the 1950s feel that the US finds so comforting. A good example of user-friendly government, and worth looking at, especially as you probably don't owe them money.

VOTESMART WEB
http://www.vote-smart.org/

This web site is in here as a lesson in democracy to other countries. No one but the Americans would have a site that tracked the performance of 13,000 elected ofiicials and gave complete backgrounds, histories and contact details. It must be murder living with truly open government. Easily accessible, well laid-out and simple to navigate, this is a beautiful site full of absolute gems – how does Daniel K. Inouye, whoever he is, feel about all his constituents knowing he didn't bother to vote on the gun control bill? E-mail him and ask.

LOCAL GOVERNMENT DIRECTORY
http://dspace.dial.pipex.com/alogic/

This site has information pages from county, city, borough and district councils in Scotland, England and Wales and links to your local authority.

SCOTTISH ENTERPRISE
http://www.scotent.co.uk/

England has TECs (Training and Enterprise Councils) but Scotland has LECs (Local Enterprise Companies) which wield a great deal of political and economic power. They come under the banner of Scottish Enterprise, the economic development agency. If you are looking for inward investment opportunities, training, business grants, encouragement for entrepreneurship etc in Scotland, start here and then find the link to your LEC.

LOCAL GOVERNMENT NETWORK FOR NORTHERN IRELAND
http://www.lgnet.org.uk/

This site contains information on all aspects of government for Northern Ireland, although a good search engine would help. But the Northern Ireland Public Service web site (http://www.nics.gov.uk/) is in many ways more comprehensive, with good links to all public service departments (education, agriculture, environment etc) in Northern Ireland.

GOVERNMENT INFORMATION IN WALES   http://www.cymru.gov.uk/

The National Assembly for Wales has comprehensive information in both English and Welsh. The newness of the site precludes a deeper assessment of its worth, but time will tell.

SCOTTISH PARLIAMENT   http://www.scottish.parliament.uk/

At the time of writing, the new Parliament in Edinburgh awaits a decent web site, but this interim version is welcome, if glitch-ridden. Seriously, if the Welsh can do it in the same time scale, what was to prevent the Scots getting their act together better?

This section has two sub-sections:

- General news – newsfeeds and dedicated news services of a general type. (More specific ones can be found in other sections.)

- Newsstand – on-line newspapers and magazines and on-line versions of paper periodicals.

Newsgroups have their own section (page 51).

General news

BBC NEWS   http://news.bbc.co.uk/

As might be expected from the world's premier news organisation, this site is up to date, well-organised and good-looking. You may never need Radio 4 again. It also links to other BBC sites such as channel information and the home page of your favourite TV programme.

NEWSHUB   http://www.newshub.com/

A real hoover of a site, NewsHub integrates and reports headlines from the world's main news sources every 15 minutes, and each section carries a tally as to how many new stories have been recently added. Therefore all stories are current. Some of it, however, is no more than press releases. Do the sources pay for this? What is clever is the fact that NewsHub is fully automated, using intelligent agent technology.

ABC NEWS   http://www.abcnews.com

Unsurprisingly US-focused, but excellent audio and video reports using Real Player. So when you have to be on-line, listen to the news at the same time.

CNN INTERACTIVE   http://www.cnn.com/

Usefully organised with good audio and video links, this site makes a feature of offering multimedia, such as interactive maps.

TOTAL NEWS　　　　　　　　http://www.totalnews.com/

With Total News Personal Edition you can create your own version of an on-line newspaper. The information you provide is analysed to help the owners sell banner adverts.

IWORLD　　　　　　　　http://www.internetnews.com

Where would a book like this be without an internet news listing? Everything you want to know about the web is here. It is interesting, though, that most news web sites look like newspapers rather than using the possibility of the web to its best advantage. This one is no exception.

Newsstand

FINANCIAL TIMES　　　　　　　　http://www.ft.com

It's pink, of course, and access is free but first-time visitors must register. You can always give false data (give your e-mail address as '@', for instance). Then there is the option to have a cookie placed on your PC 'for easy log-in'. Suspicious! Nonetheless, it is authoritative and has the option of setting up an e-mail news service. Once registered, there is an excellent link to Global Archive which has millions of articles from 3,000 newspapers world-wide, some available free.

THE GUARDIAN　　　　　　　　http://www.guardian.co.uk

The Guardian and its Sunday sister paper, *The Observer*, have a deserved reputation for design. The front page of this site is uncomplicated and pictorial. Again, access requires registration, but with options to exclude receiving information except from 'organisations carefully screened by the Guardian Media Group'. This is how such sites get paid for.

THE INDEPENDENT　　　　　　　　http://www.independent.co.uk/

When *The Indy* was launched as a paper it made a virtue out of good pictures (often, it is rumoured, to fill space in the absence of news). This site takes a similar perspective with good use of colour images. The Network section is especially good for internet-related news, features and items.

THE TELEGRAPH http://www.telegraph.co.uk

The newspaper has a reputation for being dull but worthy. This site, however, is comprehensive and attractive with a good daily index for quick browsing.

EVENING STANDARD http://www.standard.co.uk/

Many a Londoner's evening train journey home is not complete without the *Standard*. The web site is uncomplicated if slowed up by lots of Java. A particularly useful feature is the Hot Tickets what's on guide that goes beyond the newspaper's own offerings.

NEW YORK TIMES http://www.nytimes.com

Should you want US news in a format that looks like the paper it comes from, this is the site. It has everything you would expect from the grand old dame of American journalism, but (as usual) it requires registration.

USA TODAY http://www.usatoday.com

This web site is as colourful as its parent newspaper and requires no sign-in or registration. The best features are Weird News and the gloriously pictorial weather maps.

INFOJUMP http://www.infojump.com/

InfoJump is a great resource for finding past and current articles from over 3,500 magazines, newspapers, journals, newsletters and e-zines. As such, InfoJump makes a superb research tool. Whatever you want to write, rest assured somebody has written it first, and it's probably here somewhere.

NEW SCIENTIST http://www.newscientist.com

Among the first of the mainstream magazines to take the web seriously, *New Scientist* also makes a virtue of its web site by offering content additional to that available in its paper pages.

Two great features are Instant Genius (boiled-down all-you-need-to-know summaries of, say, quantum mechanics) and Last Word with answers to all those questions like: Why is the sky blue? and How do skateboarders jump their skateboards?

Getting into newsgroups is rather like going to a cocktail party for 100 million guests. The trick is to find the groups that happen to be talking about things that interest you, then move between them as the evening progresses. Unlike a party, however, internet newsgroups are organised logically and can be tracked down by their names. There are well over 25,000 newsgroups, but ranked hierarchically from starting points. These are the 10 main ones:

alt (alternative) – weirdness and a lot of 'adult' material; not for the prim.

biz (business) – commercial newsgroups, where advertising is allowed.

comp (computing) – the one for the tekkies and anoraks amongst us, with endless discussions on the relative merits of printer driver version 1.1.1.1 vs 1.1.1.0a, for instance.

news – this covers the business of newsgroups itself.

rec (recreation) – which includes sports and so on.

talk – discussion for the sake of it and a haven for insomniacs.

sci (science) – a good place to have real discussions with real scientists, this is the on-line equivalent of the scientific conference.

soc – society, culture etc.

uk – many countries have their own newsgroup hierarchy for topics of local interest (de for Germany, for instance).

misc (miscellaneous) – anything which doesn't fit anywhere else, which is hard to believe.

Below these categories the sites are named logically but in an ever-expanding tree of subdivisions separated by dots. One example from each hierarchy (see below) will give the flavour.

How to join a newsgroup

1. Check that your browser has a newsreader. Internet Explorer 3 had Internet News while the newer version 4 uses the excellent Outlook Express for news as well as e-mail and fax. Netscape has Netscape News.

2. Join your ISP's news server. The Help file with your browser will explain how to do this.

3. Subscribe to newsgroups which interest you.

A few words of warning:

- Not all ISPs carry all newsgroups – if there's a subject they don't like, they will not carry it. A lot of groups in the alt.binaries category (where the smut resides) are blocked.

- Read off-line where possible – when correctly set up, your browser will pull down any new messages in the newsgroups on your subscription list. This can take a long time if you are a member of many newsgroups, or of very popular ones. Choose a time of low phone rates, such as a weekend. Then close down your connection and read them at leisure, deciding which ones to respond to. You may need a newsreader (see FreeAgent, below).

- Read the FAQs (Frequently Asked Questions) in the newsgroup to avoid posting questions that have been answered before.

Newsgroups on the web

You can also access some news via your browser at the following:

JAMMED   http://www.jammed.com/~newzbot

Lists of newsgroups and access to recent discussions.

DEJANEWS   http://www.dejanews.com

This site carries the most recent discussions in many newsgroups.

FREEAGENT   http://www.forteinc.com/getfa/download.htm

If you do not have a newsreader, FreeAgent is excellent, free and downloadable from this web site.

A selection of newsgroups to get you started

- *alt.alien.vampire.flonk.flonk.flonk*   Oh, come now.

- *biz.marketplace.services.discussion*   A guide to transactions in the *misc.forsale.* and *biz.marketplace.* newsgroups, with suggestions for many other advertising groups.

- *comp.sys.hp.hardware*   Everything you want to know about Hewlett Packard hardware.

- *news.announce.newusers*   A good place to start. Lots of information for new users.

- *rec.aquaria.freshwater.plants*   Just what it says.

- *sci.med.prostate.prostatitis*   Including the answer to the burning question 'Is there some way to make bike riding less painful?'

- *soc.genealogy.surnames*   Starting point for discussions on name origins.

- *talk.bizarre*   Honestly, what some people do with their spare time.

- *uk.media.tv.sf.x-files*   Local fandom for the FBI Sci-Fi.

- *misc.writing.screenplays*   Instead of hanging around in Hollywood soda shops, aspiring screenwriters meet here.

Get a job! One day soon there will be no more combing of the Sunday employment supplements or local papers to see who's hiring, and no more licking envelopes containing badly printed CVs. Your updatable employment details will be available to everyone via a web database and this will be matched against jobs available. Until that happy day, here are some places to start looking.

CAREERMOSAIC http://www.careermosaic-uk.co.uk/

The UK end of this international site contains thousands of job opportunities from hundreds of employers, searchable by job title and country. Employers' Profiles has links to organisations as an aid to company research. The Career Resource Centre gives advice on CVs, covering letters and interviews plus background research on an industry or company, and hints on networking. There is a facility to post your CV on-line. A University Update page has links to UK universities on-line, plus graduate career information. There is also a USENET page to perform a full-text search of jobs listed in recruitment newsgroups. This is a thoroughly comprehensive site, well worth a visit by both job seekers and recruiters.

JOBCENTER http://www.jobcenter.com/

Excellent, attractive design marks this site out as something special. It also has on-line interviewing by videolink. You may not want to apply for any of the US hi-tech jobs on offer, but for anyone in the careers business, or considering recruitment on-line, look here to see how it should be done.

CAREER OPPORTUNITIES IN THE UK http://www.topjobs.co.uk/hayward/haywarda.htm

This well-designed, fast and exceptionally well-thought-out site can access information on a wide variety of executive career opportunities in the UK. Register a job category and region of work and be notified by e-mail when a job matching your search criteria arises. There are also links to information about the geographic area selected for job search, a useful feature if thinking of relocation.

MONSTER.COM   http://www.monster.com/

Although this is an American site, it does have international reach with job opportunities far and wide, including the UK. There are claimed to be almost 200,000 job opportunities and millions of job prospects on the database. A Job Search Agent allows you to find jobs and apply for them. There is also a CV Builder to help with applications.

PROSPECTS WEB   http://www.prospects.csu.man.ac.uk/

This is the essential guide to graduate jobs, postgraduate courses and careers information in the UK and enables students, graduates and employers to connect directly to an up-to-date on-line job match and e-mail recruitment service. Published by the Higher Education Careers Services Unit in conjunction with the Association of Graduate Careers Advisory Services (AGCAS). There are also career guides and profiles for different types of work, as well as computerised careers guidance software. Authoritative, complete and containing the latest information, it is an excellent web implementation of an excellent service.

INDUSTRY POSITIONS – MICROSOFT   http://www.careermart.com/microsoft/msjobs2.htm

Fancy a consultancy job with Microsoft based from home? Start here.

MILKROUND ONLINE   http://www.milkround.co.uk/

'The Milkround' was originally meant as a put-down for the annual trek of employers around the universities, trawling for graduates. Now it is the official title for this well-respected activity and even has its own web site. Apart from the usual job search and company profiling facilities, it has a useful Careers Advice section dealing with CVs, cover letters, interview skills, assessment centres, temping and other topics.

UNIVERSITY OF LONDON CAREERS SERVICE · http://www.careers.lon.ac.uk/

Don't be put off by the title – you may not be a student or graduate of London but this excellent site can offer help on careers-related topics, choosing a job, CVs and interviews. There is also a Careers Events listing, regularly updated part-time, temporary, voluntary and vacation jobs, a Virtual Careers Library and a growing categorised list of links to on-line careers resources. Superb!

JIIG-CAL CAREERS RESEARCH CENTRE · http://www.jiig.ed.ac.uk/

The University of Edinburgh provides a range of careers-related software, resources, information, advice and guidance. Aimed more at careers specialists and advisers, it has a wealth of useful information for job hunters. Australian version available.

THE CAREERS GATEWAY · http://www.careersoft.co.uk/

Nicely designed and fast, this comprehensive web site is aimed at UK careers, education and guidance specialists and teachers. There are also links to the web sites of professional bodies, universities and other resources to help with job finding, plus a range of useful teaching ideas and resources.

GRADUNET-VIRTUAL CAREERS OFFICE
http://www.gradunet.co.uk/scripts/webobjects.exe/gradunet.woa

This 'Virtual Careers Office' is a very cutely implemented job hunt site – and more. Good extra features include a searchable careers events list and a facility to log your spoken and written fluency in a variety of foreign languages. The geographic index is a great help and there are listings of voluntary sector jobs.

THE RECRUITMENT DATABASE · http://www.enterprise.net/recruitmentdb/

Say you are an engineer, looking for a post in the petroleum industry in the Midlands. You could post your CV on a database which employers can then search. This site provides the software (free) which allows you to upload your CV, but also has a vacancies listing and a separate area for employers, agencies, head-hunters and consultants (paid for). Database recruiting is an increasing trend and this is a good example of how it works.

SUPERMODEL   http://www.supermodel.com/

Couldn't resist it – one for the Wannabes. Everything you need to know about starting out as a professional model. They're all here: Cindy Crawford, Claudia Schiffer, Naomi Campbell, Kate Moss. You can also purchase your own official Supermodel merchandise – posters, calendars, videos, and t-shirts – and get news, gossip and so forth. Dream on!

UP FOR LEARNING   http://www.upforlearning.org.uk/

From the middle of the year 2000 the University for Industry will be a reality – a one-stop shop for all training and learning needs. The Scottish equivalent of this is currently running under a series of pilot projects, the most relevant being Napier University's South East Scotland Network (SES-NET), also known as Up for Learning. Apart from running a network of Learning Centres managed by FE colleges, the project allows direct access to a database of courses and training modules available via the web. The aim is to reach people who have never had, or never even thought of, any form of post-school education. The free Starter Packs are especially useful, and well worth signing up for. The most successful pilot in England – and still going strong – is Learning North East, based in Sunderland (http://www.learning.org.uk/).

Consult the section on filters for details of safety on the web and programs which help adults control access and content.

YAHOOLIGANS!   http://www.yahooligans.com/

The school-age version of search engine Yahoo! presents lists and links for content suitable for younger surfers, with nested categories so that children can easily find subjects of interest. There are also events and reference areas, but with a US bias. Still, it is worthwhile as a starting place for all ages.

ARGO SPHERE   http://www.argosphere.net

Activities organised by age ranges offer interactive elements for children, parents and teachers. After registration, the free part of this web site can be accessed and has a great deal of interesting and valuable content.

BUILD IT YOURSELF   http://www.build-it-yourself.com/

The official K'Nex® web site http://www.knex.co.uk/ is a disappointment but this site can't be beat for instructions on how to make toy robots, trucks, puppets and inventions using parts from LEGO®, K'nex®, electronics stores and household junk. The hope is that you will order complete kits or bits and pieces, but the plans are available free (often as downloadable zip files) and most examples should be achievable from things around the home. Einstein's Hampster House is a particular favourite.

CRAYOLA   http://www.crayola.com/index.html

The Crayola web site has been around for a while and resists the temptation to become a promotional and sales tool. It is most suitable for younger children, with parental help. This attractive site has pictures to download and colour in, games, things to make, activities and literacy aids. Parents and teachers have their own areas with useful information. For instance, explore the work of a different famous painter each week. A lot of work goes into this Web site.

DISNEY.COM
http://www2.disney.com/home/homepage/index.html

Where the Magic Lives On-line, apparently. With eveything about all aspects of Disney from Winnie the Pooh at What's on the Disney Channel to booking a cruise, the site also has good kids games and activities. Make sure your sound is turned on.

INFANT EXPLORER
http://www.naturegrid.org.uk/infant

Sebastian the Swan is your guide to literacy through stories and 'Big Books' with an environmental bent. There is a bulletin board area where e-mails can be sent and others' e-mails read. This would make a good basis for environment projects in schools. A really good feature is the Secret Agent tool which explains how to browse the site off-line, from cache memory.

KINDERART
http://www.kinderart.com/lessons.htm

This web site is huge. It contains a massive collection of artistic lessons including how to make art materials from household items and a weekly activity, quizzes and interactive elements. A great resource for art teachers in schools and a superb aid to creativity.

LEGO TRAINS BY KARL & KRISTINA BLOSS
http://www.enter.net/~bloss/lego/

People often ask 'Why would a family construct a web site?' Here's a good example. The Bloss family are clearly Lego freaks and like to share their enthusiasm. This web page is not affiliated to nor sanctioned by The LEGO® Group. But it contains all sorts of Lego-related information, construction plans and good links to other official and non-official Lego sites including http://www.lego.com.

NATIONAL GEOGRAPHIC
http://www.nationalgeographic.com/kids

A subsite of the highly recommended *National Geographic* web site, this children's area is packed with information, links to reference tools, a pen pal network, amazing facts, a cartoon factory and a games/activity area.

SCHOOLNET2000 — http://www.tesco.schoolnet2000.com

Tesco's rightly applauded 'Computers for Schools' scheme has also spun off into a project wherby computers are available in supermarkets for use by schools. This web site reflects the products of the exercise, including Millennium Files to which children can contribute.

SUPERKIDSEDUCATIONAL SOFTWARE REVIEW — http://www.superkids.com/

Really a resource of useful reviews of educational software for parents and teachers, there are links to other sites that will interest children.

TIME FOR TELETUBBIES! — http://www.bbc.co.uk/education/teletubbies/

I know. But it's popular. This site was designed by BBC Education as an aid to learning potential for pre-school children and will keep a supervised toddler amused for phone bill-stretching hours.

Consult the section on filters for details of safety on the web and programs which help adults control access and content.

INTERNET IN A BOX FOR KIDS

http://www.cnet.com/content/reviews/hands/120595/ibox.html

This product combines SurfWatch blocking software with links to sites which CompuServe thinks will appeal to 8- to 14-year-olds (see pages 106–107).

YAHOOLIGANS!

http://www.yahooligans.com/

The youth version of Yahoo! (see page 91) is a good starting place for your surfers. Also, check some of the web sites listed in Kids, Primary Age (page 58) as many of them have content suitable for older children.

ATLAPEDIA ONLINE

http://www.atlapedia.com/index.html

Visit here for information on every country in the world with facts, figures and statistics on geography, climate, people, religion, language, history and economy. A World Maps area has full colour physical and political maps.

BBC EDUCATION

http://www.bbc.co.uk/education

You can't beat the Beeb. Start at the Schools Online area with Bitesize revision help, spin off into the Learning Zone, follow up on a TV or radio programme, check out related items in the News pages and don't forget to send an e-mail to Blue Peter.

BRITANNIA

http://britannia.com/

This huge site, put together in America using UK contributors, is more fully examined in the Travel section (page 166). For schools, the History (http://britannia.com/history) and Monarchy (http://britannia.com/monarchy) sections will be especially useful, with excellent maps, timelines, features and images. Many a school project could start and finish in this site alone.

KIDSCLICK!   http://sunsite.berkeley.edu/kidsclick!/

The Berkeley Digital Library (see page 65) has catalogued more than 3,500 web resources for children, all carefully chosen, described and organised. Not to mention the cute aliens. Once you let your children near this site, you may never see them again!

MATHSNET   http://www.anglia.co.uk/education/mathsnet

Hats off to Anglia for putting together this attractive admixture of downloadable software, puzzles, games, interactive activities, feature articles and two good indexes (alphabetical and nested). Struggling with maths? Really into numbers? There is something in this web site for everyone.

THE ON-LINE BOOKS PAGE   http://www.cs.cmu.edu/bookauthors.html

Search for authors, subjects or titles for html-formatted plain ASCII text versions of classic books. This heroic undertaking by John Mark Ockerbloom of Carnegie-Mellon University deserves support as it is a good example of the excellent use to which the web can be put for educational purposes.

ROBOTS IN SPACE   http://www.brookes.ac.uk/rms/robots

Recommended for 11–13-year-olds, this sub-site of Oxford Brookes University's web site lets children explore robots, their construction and their functions in space with guidance from robots Mervyn and Robert. The site uses frames, Java and Shockwave Flash, so get the latest browser and plug-ins. Some illustrations require 3-D glasses – although there is a good explanation of how to use coloured sweet papers. Good links to other robot sites. Note that Space has its own section in this book (page 161).

CIA KIDS PAGE   http://www.odci.gov/cia/ciakids/safe.html

I just had to put it in. This is the friendly, cuddly face of the world's largest intelligence organisation with a Kid's Secret Zone. Make your own judgement.

THE ODYSSEY   http://netnow.micron.net/~odyssey/

Now here's an ambitious project. Ten travellers will visit
China, India, Iran, Egypt, Zimbabwe, Mali, Israel, Turkey and
Russia then report back to a web site accessed by, they hope,
250,000 schoolchildren. Disadvantaged children following this
'interactive world trek' on the web will follow a related
curriculum in school, and apply what they learn in their own
communities. At the time of writing, they were still seeking
some sponsorship and two additional volunteers. Check the
site to see how they're getting on.

CYBER TEEN   http://www.cteen.com/

News for teens who want to know. Parents keep out!

UNIVERSITY AND COLLEGE MAPS   http://www.scit.wlv.ac.uk/ukinfo/uk.map.html

Looking for a college or university to go to? The University of
Wolverhampton maintains a site with clickable maps of
universities, HE colleges, FE and other colleges and research
centres. Clicking takes you directly to particular places' own
web sites. A very useful resource for post-school education
generally.

Why is the sky blue? How do I get ink stains out of muslin? What is the exact meaning of 'thaumaturge'? Where can I read the complete text of *Troilus and Cressida*? Did George Washington really say 'Father, I cannot tell a lie'? (No, he didn't.) And what is a synonym for 'dyspeptic'? The web knows!

ALLEXPERTS.COM   http://www.allexperts.com/

This is the web at its best – more than 3,500 volunteer experts will answer any question on any topic. This is better than using newsgroups since posting a message doesn't always guarantee a response. But here you may ask a specific question of a specialist you select, which includes mechanics, doctors, gardeners, cooks, educationalists, travel experts and even God, apparently.

WWW VIRTUAL LIBRARY   http://www.mth.uea.ac.uk/vl

There is a nice contrast here between the 'professionals for amateurs' approach of Allexperts (above) and this 'professionals for professionals' service. Aimed at academics, it is serviced by experts who research and provide lists of key links to their areas of expertise. There are six mirror sites internationally, including the University of East Anglia, which has made a virtue of providing web-based educational resources.

PROJECT GUTENBERG   http://promo.net/pg/

There is no reason why out-of-copyright material should not be freely available on the web and the US-based project was initiated to do just that. Thousands of novels, poems and other works are here, including the Bible and Shakespeare. Searching is by title and author and quotes are easy to find. This would make a good revision aid.

ENCARTA ONLINE   http://encarta.msn.com/encartahome.asp

For those without access to Encarta (Microsoft's computer-based encyclopaedia) on CD-ROM or over a network, the 'concise' is available free with a fee-based full search option. There are puzzles, quizzes, educational games and good visuals including some 360° views.

ALT.CULTURE   http://www.altculture.com/

Youth culture is elegantly expressed in this enclyclopaedia of recent times aimed at teenagers. The design reflects the audience with bright colours, strong visuals and easy navigation – including a 'random search' feature which produces a blizzard of information. This could be just the place for parents who don't understand their children.

BARTLETT'S   http://www.columbia.edu/acis/bartleby/bartlett/

Bartlett's Familiar Quotations is so well known that Columbia University, New York, established Project Bartleby to take it (and other valuable literary and reference publications) on-line. Browsing and searching are easy and the design is simple yet effective.

BERKELEY DIGITAL LIBRARY   http://sunsite.berkeley.edu/

The combination of a large university and a large computer company ought to make for a fast and worthwhile site and that is precisely what the BDL is. Textual material, images, oral history and a wealth of other material is available from keyword searches at a remarkable speed. The site links to similar libraries around the world.

BRITISH LIBRARY   http://www.bl.uk/

The BL's web site nearly did not make it into this book – it is poorly conceived, badly implemented, slow to download the admittedly vast collection of text and images and requires the fastest and latest hardware at the user's end. A cynic would say that Magna Carta took less time to write than it does to retrieve here. There is also something counter-productive in having a web-based library catalogue which can only be searched during the library's actual opening hours. Nonetheless, it deserves to be used as it is one of our national treasures.

ENCYCLOPAEDIA BRITANNICA

http://www.eb.com/

You might expect to pay for the best, and with Britannica you would not be disappointed on either count. The charging structure is complex – day passes, monthly or yearly. The one-week free trial should give a flavour of the 70,000 articles, 10,000 illustrations and access to other resources (dictionary and biographies). The structure is pleasing and intuitive and the download speeds are acceptable.

ROGET'S THESAURUS

http//www.thesaurus.com

This is an excellent example of how having a useful publication available on-line makes it even more useful. The great utility of Roget is to use a word to find other words of similar, related or different meaning. This is so much easier by computer than on paper. Entries can be accessed alphabetically or by categories, and the Word For Today (from dictionary.com, see below) was 'emolument'. Very nice. There are also word games and crossword puzzles. If there is a criticism, it is the preponderance of adverts (which presumably pays for this worthwhile exercise), although they load fast.

DICTIONARY.COM

http://www.dictionary.com/

Apart from the expected look-up function (which annoys me, since an old teacher of mine would never tell us the spelling of a word but say 'look it up'; but if you don't know how to spell it, how do you...never mind) there is also the same Word of the Day and Crossword shared with stablemate Roget (above) and much more. This includes answers to questions about words, grammar or language, common errors in English, Strunk's Elements of Style, Bartlett's Familiar Quotations (see above) and the opportunity to delve deeper into a word with Ask Jeeves (see page 103), GoTo (http://www.goto.com/ one of the simpler search engines, see page 101), Encyclopedia.com, Infoplease, Merriam-Websters dictionary (see below for reviews of these) and good old Roget's Thesaurus. I will take this opportunity to point out that dictionary.com is the only place I have ever found a definition for 'coadunate'.

ENCYCLOPEDIA.COM　　　　　　　　　　http://www.encyclopedia.com/

I shall be in a minority of one here, but I prefer this to Britannica. It consists of 14,000 entries from the Concise Columbia Electronic Encyclopedia. Infonauts (no, it's not in dictionary.com) will admire the predictable but nicely executed book-page format which is grouped alphabetically.

INFOPLEASE　　　　　　　　　　　http://results.infoplease.com/

I adore Infoplease so much that it is now my browser's home page – in other words, it is where I start every time I fire up my web connection. Why? Because everything I ever want to know is available at this portal (see page 91). However, it is more than a portal, which is why it merits a listing here in Reference. A really useful feature is the Fact Finder with Sherlock plug-in which automatically searches for things of interest to yourself. And it has a pleasing, no-nonsense design. One to cherish.

MERRIAM-WEBSTER'S DICTIONARY　　　　　　http://www.m-w.com/

I cannot resist a dictionary with jokes. Apart from this being one of the web's best word resources, The Lighter Side of Language deserves special mention. I simply did not know that the Sanskrit root *pardate* figured in my everyday speech or that Shakespeare coined the word *leapfrog*. The design is straightforward, fast and easy on the eye. Give someone a prize, please.

THE TOLKEIN TIMELINE　　　　　　　http://gollum.usask.ca/tolkien/

J.R.R. Tolkien was a distinguished linguist and scholar as well as the greatest fantasy author. This site has a chronological list of important events in Tolkien's life, career and scholarship. Along with One Ring: The Complete Guide to Tolkien Resources (http://onering.virbius.com/), every Hobbit fan will want to have this complete guide to Tolkien information and resources on the web.

Where the web excels is in making available readily searchable database information. This is especially useful in researching public record information. There is no reason why every birth, death, marriage and baptism should not be web-available, except the time and effort it takes to input it. This is a task being steadily accomplished by enthusiasts, as is the uploading of all sorts of historical and genealogical information. Until it is all freely available there is still a need to know how to search paper-based and microfiche records, plus historical archives. For anyone interested in tracing family connections, the web has many of the sources on-line and a great deal of helpful information that points to the right places.

LATTER DAY SAINTS   http://www.familysearch.org/

If anybody is going to get genealogy right, it will be the Church of Jesus Christ of the Latter Day Saints. The Mormons believe that the dead can be saved retrospectively by claiming them as ancestors, so family histories are crucial. To this end, they have done heroic work around the world preserving, collecting, annotating and gathering together a vast array of genealogical and public records. Previously, it was necessary to visit one of their Centres. Now, at last, these resources are on-line in this beta-test version with 300 million names. Simple name searches will access a variety of databases and throw up family histories and pedigrees, including near misses, for surname variants. They all deserve sainthood, just for undertaking this mammoth, never-ending (in this life) task. The related Utah Valley Library site (http://www.lib.byu.edu/dept/uvrfhc/) has additional resources.

WHATSNEW   http://ourworld.compuserve.com/homepages/genealogy_supplies/whatsnew.htm

This is a simple but comprehensive sales site through which the various genealogy programs, record CDs and other tools and resources can be ordered. There are no downloads, but secure credit card ordering is offered.

KITH AND KIN   http://ourworld.compuserve.com/homepages/spansoft/kk.htm

One of the best genealogy software packages, Kith and Kin and the related TreeDraw are available for download as a trial version from this site, as a zip file. For every Kith and Kin registration, 50p is donated to the BDA's Diabetes 2001 fund. (In Australia and New Zealand, Kith and Kin is known as 'Of that Ilk' for legal reasons.)

FAMILYFINDER INDEX   http://www.familytreemaker.com/

In addition to a large range of record CDs for sale, there are good help and how-to resources on this site. It is less cookie-laden and ad-heavy than the better known http://www.genealogy.com/ site.

FAMILYSEARCH   http://www.lib.byu.edu/dept/uvrfhe

There is a great deal of help for beginners at the Utah Valley History Library plus links to useful sites.

Beginners

For those new to genealogy, there is a great deal of help out there.

CYNDI'S LIST   http://www.cyndislist.com

This extensive links page is alphabetically categorised and many links are annotated. Useful topic headings include countries, churches, railroads and societies.

GENHOME   http://www.genhomepage.com/full.html

This is a huge collection of links to genealogical guides, maps, software, societies and newsgroups, mostly American.

ROOT DIGGIN'   http://www.janyce.com/gene/rootdig.html

Where to start, what to avoid, tips, etiquette, and other beginners information is well organised at this site.

SUGGESTIONS FOR BEGINNERS   http://www.genealogy.org/~ngs/sugbeg.html

The National Genealogical Society's newbies' page has a good list of basic guides.

AVOIDING GENEALOGICAL GRIEF   http://www.rootsweb.com/roots-l/20ways.html

This list of twenty suggestions is good basic help for beginners to genealogical research.

GENSEARCHER   http://www.gensearcher.com

This excellent genealogical directory has access to over 150 genealogy search engines and indexes and a chat forum for researchers.

GENEALOGICAL WEB SITE WATCHDOG   http://www.ancestordetective.com/watchdog.htm

Most useful of all is this list of web sites which have misleading or inaccurate genealogical information and suggests alternatives.

Heraldry

FRANCOISVELDE'S HERALDRY SITE   http://www.heraldica.org/

This site is devoted to heraldry (the study of coats of arms) in all forms and in many different European countries. An excellent place to start in this tricky but fascinating field of study.

BLAZON   http://www.platypus.clara.co.uk/blazon.htm

Blazon is a good heraldry shareware program, very useful for producing quick visualisations of existing or new designs, and good for the beginner to heraldry.

Irish and Scots Ancestry

FIANNA GUIDE TO IRISH GENEALOGY   http://www.rootsweb.com/~fianna/

This is a great resource for anyone researching Irish ancestry.

It includes an excellent section on surnames and a good timeline of Irish history.

GATHERING OF THE CLANS   http://www.tartans.com/

You don't have to buy any tartan, most of which is an invention of Victorian romanticism. Used properly, this is the best gateway to Scottish history, culture and folklore, with access to clan sites and a good section on Scottish heraldry and, of course, tartans.

There is something vaguely paradoxical about finding out about fitness while sitting in a chair staring at a monitor, but then, it is equally weird to sit in an armchair with a big box of chocolates and watch Jane Fonda workout videos. If your heart's desire is to discover how to be healthy from the comfort of your computer room, start with these excellent sites.

ALCOHOL CONCERN   http://www.alcoholconcern.org.uk

It would be easy for a site like this to come over all stern advice and finger-wagging. In fact, it is down to earth and sympathetic with good fact sheets, links and information. The design is basic (using standard Microsoft clipart) but the navigation is straightforward – you won't get lost in it.

THE ALTERNATIVE GUIDE   http://www.altguide.com

This is the on-line version of the *Alternative Guide to Complementary Health and Healing in London and the South of England* seen in healthfood shops and other stores. Although biased to the London area (especially the What's On, Daily Listings and links to Therapists), it has generally useful information on everything from Acupuncture to Zone Therapy (taking in Laughter Therapy on the way).

FITNESS ONLINE   http://www.fitnessonline.com/

Someone has thought long and hard about this site – attractive, navigation by drop-down lists and clickable images and some unparalleled content. The Workouts section contains information sheets, searchable by the part of the body you most need to shape up. And if you want to amuse your friends, there is a facility to e-mail the pages to them – How To Shape Up Your Bottom should go down well. This is one of a 'nest' of online fitness mags, including Shape, Flex, Mens Fitness and Fit Pregnancy, all available via this site.

FRAGRANT AT DEMON   http://www.fragrant.demon.co.uk/

Graham Sorenson's basic but unpretentious framed site is a

good example of an individual using the web to promote an interest, hobby or business. It contains a list of UK aromatherapy practitioners and suppliers, a database with photos of people in aromatherapy, descriptions of the oils used, a Symptoms Guide, Glossary, Events and a large annotated list of 600 other aromatherapy sites. Clearly a work of love.

KIDSHEALTH.ORG   http://kidshealth.org/

For kids, health is boring! However, the paediatric specialists at the Alfred I. duPont Hospital for Children in Florida understand this and have put together an excellent, attractive web site packed with information on infections, behaviour, emotions, food and fitness, and growing up healthy. They obviously understand children, as the games and animations show. A train theme leads to hundreds of articles and to-do features. If your kids must spend all their time and your phone bills playing net games, try them on this site and they might learn something. Sub-sites for parents and teenagers are also worth a visit.

PARASOL EMT   http://www.parasolemt.com.au/

This is an on-line first aid information and advice guide from Parasol, an Australian commercial training provider of first aid and health and safety training. It is focuses on Australia, with a large section on snakebites, but then eleven of the world's twelve most venomous reptiles live there. Sensible, pragmatic advice, easily searchable.

THE SERGEANT'S PROGRAM   http://www.sarge.com/

Nicely conceived, this on-line version of a popular American fitness programme invites you to sign up for torture sessions at a fitness camp run on army lines, none in the UK, thankfully. This site is a good example of taking a single motif and designing a web site around it. Some limited on-line advice on exercise. Will I be joining? Sir, no Sir!

THRIVE ONLINE   http://www.thriveonline.com/

This US site is a straightfoward, no-nonsense Consumer Health web-site packed with information on medicine, fitness, sports, diet and what they coyly call 'passion'. On-line exercises, diets, medical advice etc are worthwhile. Clear design and multiple navigation options add to the site's appeal.

THE TOOTH FAIRY   http://www.toothfairy.org/

Actually a site of links to other dental hygeine sites, this nicely-designed site is another good example of an individual taking an obesssion on-line. It provides access to a wealth of information on teeth and tooth matters. I had no idea that oral disease was recently shown to be the number one health problem diagnosed in dogs and cats. In the USA, perhaps.

TRASHED   http://www.trashed.co.uk/audio/index.html

The Health Education Authority (HEA) used to be a worthy but boring organisation which tried to get us all to eat, behave and live more sensibly. A few years ago they would never have done (or been allowed to do) anything like Trashed. This is video-enabled, sound-enabled, in-your-face information about drugs – their effects, the law, what's in them, emergencies and the risks. Trashed looks and feels like a rock video – they know their audience. A specially neat touch is the ability to tell them a new 'street' name for a banned substance, so others can look it up. The larger HEA web site (http://www.hea.org.uk/) is dull and not a patch on the Scottish version (see HebsWeb, below).

HEBSWEB   http://www.hebs.scot.nhs.uk/

One day, all health sites will be like this. Conceived for and aimed at Scotland's appalling health problems, there is nonetheless something here for everyone – smoking, heart disease, healthy eating. There is an excellent Videowall facility (which requires a plug-in or ActiveX control that will probably be part of the latest browser versions) and some of the site is for the health professions only. But the vast majority is accessible, useful, sobering and well-implemented.

PHARMWEB   http://www.pharmweb.net/

This is a web site for professionals – pharmacists, doctors and others – and a lot of the information is technical and in depth. But for the general public there is an amazing amount of information on drugs and medicines. It is simply designed and easy to navigate if somewhat hard to read in places.

RXLIST   http://www.rxlist.com/

This is really an on-line pharmacy – buy medicine over the internet – but it also has a good deal of patient information, a searchable database of drugs and their indications and interactions and even 'RxLaffs', a gloriously unfunny comic strip. There is good coverage of herbs, homeopathics, Chinese medicines and Ayurvedic therapies.

PATIENT INFORMATION   http://www.patient.co.uk/

It's your body, after all, so you should find out as much as possible about it. This is the place to start. There are about 20 categories of information and a wealth of links to other resources. As an exercise in collecting together and codifying the bewildering amount of information out there on the web, this site is truly excellent and devoid of pretentions.

AIDSMAP   http://www.aids.map.com/

Anyone who is confused about HIV and AIDS, prevention, treatment and myth-busting should begin with this site from a consortium of official and semi-official bodies. The design is taken from the London Underground map and makes for easy navigation through a mass of complex but plain-language detail. This is a good example of a site where as much thought has gone into how to make information readily available as into the information itself, which is a welcome rarity.

THE NHS   http://www.nhs50.nhs.uk/

To celebrate its 50th anniversary, the National Health Service has developed this rich and interesting site. There is a treasure store of historical detail and good information downloads for schools. The photographic collections are worthwhile in their own right.

CDC   http://www.cdc.gov/

The Centers for Disease Control and Prevention is America's (and to some extent the world's) watchdog on diseases, their spread and their control. The best feature of the site is its extremely comprehensive searchable database which produces technical and up-to-date references (some in Adobe Acrobat pdf format) on almost any disease. The travellers' health tips are also extremely good if somewhat alarmist in a well-meaning way. It's interesting that they consider the greatest risks to health in Serbia/Montenegro are travellers' diarrhoea and malaria.

MEDSCAPE   http://www.medscape.com/index.html

If you want to annoy your GP, print out everything there is to know on any condition from a Medline search of the latest journals and go armed with the information. This is a professionals' site available to the public if you register. There is also an accessible Patient Information section.

The web has opened up a brave new world to everyone with an obsession and the desire to share it widely. There is a vast profusion of pet-related sites out there, most of them extremely dismal. However, apart from the usual 'this is a nice picture of my puppy' and the huge collection of commercial organisations eager to sell you ever-better ways to placate your guppies, there are some good places to go for advice on cute kittens or happy hamsters and some genuinely thoughtful sites about animal welfare.

PETS ON THE INTERNET   http://www.acmepet.com/

This is a commercial site, but it is packed with good information on all pets, especially cats, dogs, birds, horses, fish and what it coyly calls 'exotics'. Help – My Lizard Won't Eat is a typical example.

PETS CORNER   http://www.catholic.org.uk/kidz_stuff/under_13/pets_corner/default.htm

This is a good site for kids (organised by age ranges) on the care and feeding of pets. A real vet answers questions. The site has undertones of organised religion trying to be useful.

AAAAAARGH. THE RATZ!   http://www.ratz.co.uk/

Pests to some, pets to others, rats are enjoying unprecedented popularity. This site has exclusively UK content and deals with all aspects of rodent care. RatCam is a good idea.

ANIMAL AID ONLINE   http://www.animalaid.org.uk/

This animal rights campaign site deals with anti-vivisection, animal experimentation, factory farming and vegetarianism. It is well-organised and easy to navigate with a good educational section which makes up in enthusiasm what it lacks in balance.

AQUASOURCE   http://www.aquasource.demon.co.uk/

Although an on-line pet supplies site, Aquasource is also a good repository of information on aquaria, fish in general and other related topics. The arcade games are amusing.

NETVET
http://netvet.wustl.edu/vet.htm

This site is a testament to the late night web-surfing of vet Ken Boschert from St Louis, Missouri. It is possibly the most thorough resource on the web for all aspects of animal care. If you can't find it here, it probably doesn't exist. He has also developed a superb Electronic Zoo (http://netvet.wustl.edu/e-zoo.htm).

BACHMAN KIDDENS' CATCYCLOPEDIA
http://209.1.224.11/~sniksnak/catcyclopedia.html

Everything about cats, in an A–Z format, with cute music to accompany the loading.

UK CAT BREEDERS
http://www.palantir.co.uk/breeder.html

The GCCF maintains this site about pedigree cats in the UK with lists of breeders, cat clubs and cat shows plus breed information and standards of points.

DOGS ON-LINE
http://www.dogsonline.co.uk/

Good dog-related sites are extremely rare on the Web, whereas cat sites abound. Is this a measure of how much spare time the respective owners have? Dogs on-line was the UK's first on-line dog magazine just for dog lovers – originally supported by The Princes Trust – and is still the best forum for articles, news, breeder lists, products, dog rescue information and directories of kennels, dog clubs and animal-friendly accommodation. The design is simple but effective.

PIGS AS PETS
http://www.gulfaccess.net/ofcmgmt/papa_archives/desktop.htm

Dedicated to the pot-bellied pig and its place in the household, this eccentric web site deals with all aspects of the care of porkers. Even if you never intend to have one around the house, do take a look. The fake Windows Desktop is an inspiration.

VETPEDIA
http://www.pathfinder.com/petpath/vetpedia/index.vp.html

Search this database for help with routine care of cats and dogs. Find out about specific problems and treatment.

VIRTUAL CREATURES
http://www.virtualcreatures.com/vc/index.html

What will the virtual pets of the future look and sound like? This site is actually a showcase for design company Global Beach. Download the Chilean Rose Tarantula, watch it grow and develop over about three weeks, then be grateful it lives behind your monitor screen.

Internet shopping is big business. In 1998 over £4 billion was spent on-line and about half of the UK's eight million web users have ordered and paid for something via the web or using e-mail. Some of the large high street shops such as Tesco, Sainsbury's and Dixons/Curry's and major retailers like Dell Computers and Elonex have major direct-sale web presences and are devoting more and more of their resources to the virtual supermarket. Why is this so popular all of a sudden?

Saving money

Without the need to maintain expensive buildings or employ staff to stock shelves, deal with customers and handle goods, a virtual shop can be remarkably cost-effective. This is even more the case when the virtual shop has no stock to carry – by reselling goods from the manufacturer without having to warehouse them. Lower costs means higher margins and this means reduced prices to the customer. Books or CDs ordered on-line can be as much as 40 per cent cheaper, even with the postage and packing charge.

Saving time

It is, in theory, far quicker to find a book at Amazon or a CD at CD Now, order and pay for it on-line, than to visit a physical shop to make the purchase. This is not always the case – you may be out shopping anyway – and there is the important 'window shopping element' of visiting the shopping mall or high street, which many people enjoy. In addition, many prefer the immediacy of actual purchase. However, there is a rising trend towards browsing in 'real' shops, deciding on the purchase, then actually completing it at home on the web, thus saving money.

Saving effort

Not only are on-line shops easier to browse than, say, paper catalogues, the purchase itself does not require manual form-filling with a pen and posting via the mail. In many systems, once you are known and have your details stored, repeat purchases can be one or two mouse clicks away. Standing orders for groceries are becoming more popular, with delivery in certain areas. On-line is the ideal way to buy something that itself can be delivered on-line – information, documents and software are obvious examples.

Shop internationally

Not many of us get the chance to hit Macy's in New York, but they will dispatch on-line orders to the UK, albeit with shipping charges and any import duty added. It's still cheaper than a plane ticket.

Security

'Are my credit card details safe?' is the major concern of prospective on-line shoppers. According to booksellers Amazon, there has not been a single case of fraud reported by any of their 6 million customers. In fact, credit card transactions via the web are in many ways more secure than handing over your card in a restaurant. The merchant usually never sees your credit card number and only has access to the last four digits – the rest is handled by the transaction processer and verified by the bank. However, it is only sensible to take the same precautions as you would when using a card in a shop, namely:

- Buy from places you trust – Boots, Dixons and Virgin are likely to be as concerned over your on-line consumer rights as if you were standing in their shops. Alternatively, Shop Safe (http://www.shopsafe.co.uk/) and ShopGuide (http://www.shopguide.co.uk/) have links to known brands and BarclaySquare (http://www.barclaysquare.com/) takes you to sites Barclaycard recommends.

- Keep a record of your purchase.

- Check your credit card statement.

- Inform your card issuer if there are any unauthorised transactions and your liability will be limited to £50, just as for normal transactions.

In addition, there are web-specific security measures:

- Make sure the web site you order from uses Secure Socket Layers (SSL) which encrypts your information. If your browser shows the SSL icon (a small key in Internet Explorer and a padlock in

Netscape), then it is secure.

- Deal with a company which offers a security guarantee – if your card details are used by another person without your permission, they will refund any money not covered by your card issuer. Mastercard has the ShopSmart system of standards (http://www.mastercard.com/shopsmart/) which on-line traders must comply with.

- Buy from a company which uses one of the Certificate systems – the industry body TrustE (http://www.truste.org/) and Verisigns WebTrust (http://www.verisign.com/webtrust/) verify and certificate on-line shops – and which have a clear statement on security in the web site.

- Use on-line shops which have some form of order confirming and tracking system and contact details (address and/or phone number) so that you can get in touch if there are problems.

Understand the issues

The UK government report on on-line shopping in the DTI Secure Electronic Commerce Statement (http://www.dti.gov.uk/CII/ana27p.html) makes interesting reading for anyone who wishes to take this further. Actinic Software (http://www.actinic.co.uk/) offers web security tools. NetBanx (http://www.netbanx.com/) has information about on-line banking info. The Multicards site (http://www.multicards.com/) is the best source for a wealth of information on credit card transactions. Both the American National Fraud Information Center (http://www.fraud.org/) and the UKs Financial Services Authority (http://www.fsa.gov.uk/) have the facts on the regulation of e-commerce, the real extent of e-fraud and other important matters. Trade Law (http://www.tradelaw.com/) is a site which deals with issues relating to customs and import fees.

Make your views known

Many sites carry reviews of products – particularly books and music – to which you can add your own thoughts. Some sites encourage you to e-mail the vendor and ask questions to put your mind at ease, a good example being gourmet@jayfruit.co.uk. (see below under Food, page 85).

Find a bargain

Some sites exist specifically to find the lowest price – travel deals are dealt with on page 164, but Bottom Dollar or Excites Product Finder (see below) will search the web according to your requirements and find the best price. Some sites will e-mail you when an item becomes available – like a new CD or the latest version of software.

Make money

If you have a web site of your own, become a reseller – simply by putting a link from your page to Amazon, CD Now or many other on-line shops, you could receive a percentage, sometimes as much as 15 per cent, of a purchase initiated through your site. You never have to handle the goods or the payment mechanism, just sit back and wait for the cheque. There is an example of an on-line mall, specifically created for this book, at http://www.fifeweb.net/shops/ and all proceeds go nowhere near any charity. There are numerous e-shopping creation programs, but **SHOPCREATOR** (http://www.shopcreator.com/) and **INTERSHOP** (http://www.intershop.com/) are fair examples to help you set up your own e-shop. Increasingly, ISPs and web hosting services are offering e-commerce options, though usually via their sites and in a non-flexible way.

Supermarkets

TESCO (http://www.tesco.co.uk/) and **SAINSBURY** (http://www.sainsbury.co.uk/) offer on-line groceries and more, but their intentions are different. Tesco plans to extend its M25 area delivery service to all parts of the country, but Sainbury's site means to tempt you to visit the shop. A relatively new service from **WAITROSE** called Waitrose@work will deliver groceries to a workplace, if the employer organises the scheme (http://www.waitrose.com/).

High Street Retailers

BOOTS (http://www.boots.co.uk/) and **DIXONS/CURRY'S** (http://www.dixons.com/) are the best-known examples and their sites are well laid out, easy to navigate and simple to use.

On-line Malls

VIRTUAL SHOPPING (http://www.comlab.ox.ac.uk/archive/other/shopping.html) has the best set of links to the growing number of these e-shopping centres. The above-mentioned MaxShop, Shop Safe and ShopGuide are also good places to start.

Music

HMV (http://www.hmv.co.uk/) has a good on-line version of its stores, but other music dealers exist. Among the best are **IMVS** (http://www.musicandvideo.co.uk/), **THE INTERNET MUSIC SHOP** (http://www.musicsales.co.uk/), **PRIDE RECORDS** (http://www.priderecords.co.uk/) and, best known of all, **CD NOW** (http://www.cdnow.com/). **W H SMITH** has a CD division on-line (http://www.cdparadise.com/) and the UK version of **AUDIOSTREET.COM** (http://www.audiostreet.co.uk/) is worth a visit. **OUR PRICE** (http://www.our-price.com/) sells CDs as well as videos and books, but via the US-based Amazon.com which is not always the most useful for UK purchasers.

Films

REEL COM (http://www.reel.com/) and the **INTERNET MOVIE DATABASE** (http://www.imdb.com/) combine good review sections with ordering facilities. **DVDPLUS** (http://www.dvdplus.co.uk/) and **BLACK STAR** (http://www.blackstar.co.uk/) are good sources of movies on video and DVD.

Books

AMAZON (http://www.amazon.co.uk/ or http://www.amazon.com/ for non-UK books) have reviews and a simple ordering mechanism, plus a book search facility that can track down rare, out of print or hard to find volumes. Not all UK books are known to **AMAZON.COM** and not all foreign books to **AMAZON.CO.UK**, so use both if necessary. **BARNES AND NOBLE** (http://www.barnesandnoble.com/) are finding to their cost that as their web site becomes more popular, their street-front bookshops are losing custom. **CITRON PRESS** (http://www.citronpress.co.uk) sells its authors' books via Amazon, but also offers the opportunity to get your own masterpiece published. Other useful and well-thought-out sites are **THE BOOK PEOPLE** (http://www.thebookpeople.co.uk/), **BOOKS ON LINE** (http://www.bol.com), **DILLONS** (http://www.dillons.co.uk/), **HEFFERS** (http://www.heffers.co.uk/),

PENGUIN (http://www.penguin.co.uk/) and **WATERSTONE'S ONLINE**
(http://www.waterstones.co.uk/).

Classified ads

LOOT (http://www.loot.com) costs £1.25 to read but has hundreds if not
thousands of second-hand bargains, easily searchable by
keyword. **NET CLASSIFIEDS** (http://www.ltnol.com) operates much the
same way. **EXCHANGE AND MART** (http://www.exchangeandmart.co.uk/) is
hanging in there. But here you will be paying some third party,
so keep a record and make sure you know what you are getting,
as with any purchase from the classifieds in a newspaper.

International and Designer shopping

BRAS DIRECT (http://www.brasdirect.co.uk/bras/) is the place for ladies' lingerie
and **CHARLES TYRWHITT** (http://www.ctshirts.co.uk/) for gents' shirts. Friends
of Flat Eric can get their jeans direct from **LEVI** (http://www.eu.levi.com/)
but can also exercice choice at **DIESEL UK** (http://www.diesel.co.uk) and, for
more clothing items in general, **GAP** (http://www.gap.com/) and
NORDSTROMS (http://www.nordstroms.com/) which has a particularly good
Sale section. **FAO SCHWARTZ** (http://www.faoschwartz.com/), the famous Fifth
Avenue (and 37 other locations) toyshop, and **MACY'S**
(http://www.macys.com/) are your Manhattan transfer for cosmopolitan
shopping. More down to earth, **SCOTIA** (http://www.scotia.uk.com/) has a
decent range of outdoor wear for those days when web-surfing
pales.

Specialist items, Food and Drink

THE CLASSIC ENGLAND SHOPPING MALL
(http://www.classicengland.co.uk/) sells those uniquely British knick-
knacks which only American tourists buy, but also everything
English from cloth caps to cough sweets and historic newspapers
(http://www.classicengland.co.uk/historic.html) with back issues to 1810.
WINE CELLAR UK (http://www.winecellar.co.uk/) is a reasonable on-line
vintners as is **CHATEAU ONLINE** (http://www.chateauonline.co.uk/).
THORNTONS ONLINE (http://www.thorntons.co.uk/) will supply chocoholics
with the needful and **JAYFRUIT** (http://www.jayfruit.co.uk/) has le
gourmet français and gorgeous delicatessen products by mail. As
you would expect, **FORTNUM AND MASON** (http://www.fortnumandmason.co.uk/)
has absolutely everything, except perhaps a Web cam in the tea

room to watch Adam Faith have his daily cuppa.

Auctions

These are becoming increasingly common. The recognised leader is **EBAY** (http://www.ebay.com/) which has the added advantage of including buyers comments. **QXL** (http://www.qxl.co.uk/) is also worthwhile. Just as for classifieds (see above, page 85), the vendor is not the site host, but a third party, so take the same safeguards. Often auction links will pop up on search engine and other sites and lead you to pages with apparently excellent bargains which do not, in any real sense, exist – they are a marketing trick to get you to a particular site.

Seek and find

For bargain hunters, **EXCITE'S PRODUCT FINDER** (http://www.jango.com/xsh/index.dcg?) and **BOTTOM DOLLAR** (http://www.bottomdollar.com/) will search for the best price for any item or service and present you with a list of dealers with clickable links to their own pages. This is particularly useful for items which might be available from a variety of dealers – computers would be a good example – but at wildly differing prices. Let the bargain finders do the hard work.

Cars

See the motoring section (page 136) for new and used car sales sites, but start with **AUTOLOCATE** (http://autolocate.uk.msn.com/).

Computers

Not surprisingly, computer manufacturers are switched on to the possibility of e-sales, and have turned their mail-order and direct sales businesses into web shops. Among the best known are **DABS DIRECT** (http://www.dabs.com/), **DAN TECHNOLOGY** (http://www.dan.co.uk/), **DELL** (http://www.dell.co.uk/), **ELONEX** (http://www.elonex.co.uk/), **EVESHAM MICROS** (http://www.evesham.com/), **INSIGHT** (http://www.insight.com/uk/), **PICO DIRECT** (http://www.picodirect.co.uk/) and **TECH DIRECT** (http://www.techdirect.co.uk/).

Games and software

Apart from the sites in the sections on games (page 24) and

software (page 29), try **GAME RETAIL** (http://www.game-retail.co.uk/) who will e-mail you when new versions of your chosen software are available.

This could be a book in itself. Therefore it is a very selective list. Each site is a good starting point when searching for information on aspects of PC computing and the web. Other sections cover software download sites and different aspects of computing. This is a catch-all.

LEARNINGHTML   http://www.bev.net/computer/htmlhelp/

This is not a great site in itself. It breaks Rule 1 (don't use white text on black because some browsers may not display the black) and Rule 2 (slabby text is boring) but it represents quite a lot of hard work. It has excellent links to lots of other resources which contain everything you need to know about designing web sites plus all the software you need to get started. A good place to begin.

DRIVERGUIDE.COM   http://www.driverguide.com/

There are few things more frustrating than not having the right driver for your new printer, scanner, sound card etc. This site, a guide to finding drivers on the internet, has them all, nicely structured and usually with installation instructions. Registration is required.

PC COMPUTING   http://www.zdnet.com/~pccomp/

Out of the ZDNet stable, this is one of the best and most reliable of the on-line PC magazines, and also looks good. This particular section is one of the Insider Secrets sections put together by the magazine staff. It goes beyond the usual lists and links format to offer sensible, sage, well-reasoned advice on many aspects of computing and related matters, including tips, hints and tricks not found (easily) anywhere else.

BRILLIANET   http://www.brillianet.com/programming/

Attractive, understated and unpretentious, this web site provides access to first-steps programming guides, reference manuals, examples and tutorials for Assembler, C/C++ , IPX Network JavaScripting and Turbo Pascal. There is also a list of programs and utilities by the authors.

FAQS BY CATEGORY   http://www.lib.ox.ac.uk/internet/news/faq/by_category.index.html

If any one organisation had a claim to know everything, it might well be Oxford University. This page contains answers to frequently asked questions taken from over 1,000 newsgroups. The subject matters go from A to Zoroastrianism. Search by newsgroup or via an Excite-based search engine. The computing-related links are particularly useful.

FAQ FINDER   http://ps.superb.net/faq/

This site allows the surfer to search for Frequently Asked Questions by name or category from about 1,800 FAQs. It has a very simple user interface which makes navigation quick and pleasurable.

WINDOWS 95 FAQS   ftp://rtfm.mit.edu/pub/usenet/comp.os.ms-windows.win95.misc/

Everybody has questions about Windows 95 (mostly, 'Why won't it work?'). This compilation of FAQs from the comp.os.ms-windows.win95.misc newsgroup, usually has, or can get you to, an authoritative answer faster than Microsoft on-line support. It is an FTP site, so there is no navigation as such. But it is packed with useful things and also has some amusing exchanges between antagonists and links to other informational web sites.

HELP-SITE COMPUTER MANUALS   http://help-site.com/

Trying to use software somebody 'lent' you? Lost the manual? This is an inspired idea – links to 365 on-line manuals and tutorials about DOS, Windows, internet, networking, Unix and programming. Some of the documents are in Abobe (pdf) format, so you need to download Acrobat Reader before you can open any documents. A clever aspect of this site is that it uses a database to generate each page on demand. This makes it faster and more flexible. It also has links to many other computer-related sites. The site is selective about accepting submissions, so there is very little dross.

MATT'S SCRIPT ARCHIVE
http://scriptarchive.com/

This is the only place to get tried and tested cgi scripts and programming tools to make your web site zing and hum. The related CGI Resource Index (http://www.cgi-resources.com/) has over 1,200 cgi resources listed!

Directories are not the same as search engines, although they usually include these. If you don't mind someone else's ideas of what sites to be sent to (which often comes down to who has paid to be there rather than what is good or useful), then a portal is as fine a place to start as any.

Portals are web pages with, in theory, everything on them that you would need – navigation, news, TV listings, searches – and a place to start your web-surfing. They take the guesswork out of finding the right place to go first. Web rings are virtual communities with interlinked navigation so that, once in a ring, you can surf around in it or even ask for a random link. Rings bring together visitors, member sites and advertisers/merchants, and so remain free of charge to visitors and members. Many users set up their internet browser to recognise one of these directories as a home page. The directory then appears everytime you open the internet. Instructions to help you do this are as follows:

- Netscape 4 Edit, Preferences, Navigator, Navigator starts with Home Page, Use current page.

- Internet Explorer 4 View, Internet Options, General, Home Page, Use Current.

YAHOO!   http://www.yahoo.com

Yahoo!, which more or less invented this area of web activity, classifies its sites into rather broad groupings (Arts and Humanities, Business and Economy, Computers and Internet, Education, Entertainment, Government, Health, News and Media, Recreation and Sports, Reference, Regional, Science, Social Science, Society and Culture) but hierarchically from there on in. A useful twist is the ability to specify your country and even your region so the searches are more specific to your locale.

MINING CO   http://www.miningco.com

The Mining Company claims to take the hard graft out of finding a *good* web site by including sites which have been reviewed by, and are introduced by, a 'guide' qualified in that area of expertise. In addition, the design is excellent and the navigation intuitive.

VIRTUAL LIBRARY
http://celtic.stanford.edu/vlib/overview.html

As befits a major seat of learning, Stanford University has put together a good library of sites (in roughly the same categories as Yahoo! above). To save your browsing time, there are mirror sites in various locations, including the UK. It is, of course, simply a list of links (or more properly access to about 300 other virtual libraries). But it is cleverly structured so that if you wanted, say, access to a database of web-accessible material on computational linguistics and natural-language processing, it would be obvious how and where to get to it within two or three mouse clicks. There is also both an alphabetical listing and a keyword search, plus the ability to add your own or favourite virtual library, subject to their verification and approval. This is what local branch libraries are up against unless they embrace the concept themselves.

WEBRING
http://www.webring.org

Clearly not designed by a librarian (in that it actually has a good design) the WebRing gives access to hundreds of thousands of member web sites organised by interest groupings called 'rings'. Navigation is by subject directory or a search engine. Once into a WebRing member page, navigation buttons or links take you to other sites in that ring. It isn't selective, like Stanford's VL (above), as anyone can apply to join a ring or create a new site. However, they will deny service to anyone or suspend a ring if the system is being 'abused'. The directory is called – wouldn't you know it – Ringworld, doubtless managed by Ringmasters. WebRing has 500,000 daily visitors and 500,000 member sites in 40,000 rings.

SIX DEGREES
http://www.sixdegrees.com/affiliate/index.asp?affiliateid=428

Sean MacManus is the portals guru. To prove it, he has constructed a portal site, based on the theory that no one is more than six degrees of separation away from anyone else. As befits his knowledge and status, Sean has put together a really good starting place for all your web needs and foibles, including a daily poll. Do you wish your hair was: straight, curly, wavy? Forty-seven per cent chose straight!

RESEARCH IT   http://www.itools.com/research-it/

This site takes a different tack and assumes that sometimes what you want is not a web site link, but an answer. Organised very nicely into six broad categories (Language, Library, Geographical, Financial, Shipping and Internet), this site takes you directly, by keyword, to useful research tools such as dictionaries, translators, maps and phone books. Check out the CIA's World Factbook. If they don't know, who does? They don't know Scotland exists, which is fine by me. But did you know that in 1998 the UK had 12,069,296 males fit for military service? The CIA did. Spooky!

INFOJUMP   http://www.infojump.com/

See the News section (page 47) for more details.

There's no reason why anyone should have to pay for internet access other than the cost of a local phone call via an 0845 number.

The Internet Service Providers (ISPs) listed below all offer free 0845 access and, in many cases, free e-mail and web space as well.

There must be a catch – but there isn't. These ISPs make money in two ways – from support numbers charged at BT premium rate and a share of BT's charges from the 0845 number.

Signing up to an account is usually extremely easy and there is the added advantage that if one fails to please you, just change – bearing in mind that your e-mail address may not be portable.

Support

If you think you'll need a lot of support, choose an ISP which gives it cheap or free rather than one which charges premium rates. There has been something of a price war in the support line charges recently, with Dixon's Freeserve dropping its £1 per minute charge to 50p in the light of Tesco's imminent arrival on the free ISP scene. Do note that some offer free support on-line or by e-mail. Some also close from midnight until early morning – usually the time you need support most, when it all goes horribly wrong in the wee small hours. A good choice on this basis is **Free4All**.

More experienced users may choose one which offers large amounts of free web space for that life-size jpeg of your train set, additional e-mail addresses and different forms of support. I personally use **ConnectFree** and have rarely had to engage their support. It is a measure of the adequacy of their service (and my inertia) that I have not moved to another ISP.

ISP is not the same as dial-up

There is nothing to stop you having your dial-up with one of these and your web site hosted elsewhere, with your e-mail from somewhere else entirely. This is useful if you have taken one of these 'e-mail address for life' packages, such as **Yahoo!** or **Netscape** offer, but use your free dial-up to access the service.

Listings may change

The list below is alphabetical, except that those offering free support are listed first and premium line support providers last. As ever, bear in mind that this information is correct at the time of writing but may change. Free support is becoming the norm. It remains to be seen whether this affects the quality and speed of the support offered.

CONNECTFREE   http://www.connectfree.co.uk

Free web space – unlimited; e-mail addresses – unlimited; support – free on-line.

FREE2U   http://www.free2you.co.uk

Free web space – yes; e-mail addresses – yes; support – free by e-mail, free on-line.

FREE4ALL   http://www.free4all.co.uk

Free web space – 10Mb; e-mail addresses – unlimited POP; support – 8am–midnight local phone rates, free on-line.

BREATHE   http://www.timetobreathe.net

Free web space – 10Mb; e-mail addresses – 5; support – 24-hour premium phone rates.

FREE-INTERNET   http://www.free-internet.co.uk

Free web space – 10Mb; e-mail addresses – 1 POP; support – 24-hour premium phone rates, free by e-mail, free on-line.

FREE-ONLINE   http://www.free-online.net

Free web space – unlimited; e-mail addresses – unlimited, 5 POP; support – 7am–11pm premium phone rates, free by e-mail, free on-line.

FREENET   http://www.freenet.co.uk

Free web space – 20Mb; e-mail addresses – unlimited POP; support – premium phone rates, free by e-mail, free on-line.

FREESERVE   http://www.freeserve.net

Free web space – 15Mb; e-mail addresses – unlimited; support
– 24-hour premium phone rates, free by e-mail, free on-line.

FREEUK   http://www.freeuk.com

Free web space – 25Mb; e-mail addresses – unlimited; support
– 24-hour premium phone rates, free by e-mail.

FREEWAY UK   http://www.freewayuk.com

Free web space – 20Mb; e-mail addresses – unlimited; support
– 24-hour premium phone rates.

UK FANTASTIC   http://www.ukfantastic.net

Free web space – 5Mb; e-mail addresses – unlimited POP;
support – 24-hour premium phone rates, free on-line.

VIRGIN   http://www.virgin.net

Free web space – 10Mb; e-mail addresses – yes; support – 24-
hour premium phone rates, free by e-mail, free on-line.

Free e-mail addresses

Free e-mail is also becoming popular and many ISPs offer a
certain number (often 5, but sometimes unlimited). Why would
you need more than one? For instance, a small company might
need one per employee or a home user one for each family
member. Usually, an e-mail account is easy to set up with
software configuration done over the web (known as webmail).

In these cases you will be stuck with the host's domain name
– if you are M. Mouse your e-mail address from Freethingy may
become mmouse@freethingy.net, but if you have also taken some web
space you may get a virtual domain to yourself, with a name you
choose, such as mousehole (mmouse@mousehole.freethingy.net).

The companies below do not offer dial-up, but will give you
free e-mail. In each case, a typical e-mail address is given for the
fictitious M. Mouse.

Yahoo!	http://mail.yahoo.com
web-based	mmouse@yahoo.com
Hotmail	http://www.hotmail.com
web-based	mmouse@hotmail.com
Mail.com	http://www.mail.com
web-based	mmouse@mail.com

To do any serious web browsing, there are some absolute essentials. These are listed below, with download sites where they can be obtained.

Version 4 browsers

By a coincidence, Netscape brought out Netscape Communicator 4.0 around the same time as Internet Explorer 4.0, both of which had added functionality, such as the ability to run Java (a programming language which extends the browser's capacity to do interesting things) and ActiveX (Microsoft's add-ins to enable sound, video etc). These are therefore called Version 4 browsers and it is worth downloading and installing them if your browser is an earlier version. How to check? If you have Netscape or Internet Explorer click <u>H</u>elp <u>A</u>bout and there will be a version number. At the time of writing the latest versions were Netscape 4.51 and Explorer 4.1

NETSCAPE	http://home.netscape.com/comprod/mirror/index.html

Start here to download or upgrade Netscape and – cheekily – learn how to uninstall Internet Explorer. It is possible to get lost in Netscape's complicated site, so start here. And if you sign on to receive updates and news, you'll be bombarded with information and offers. Still, why not?

INTERNET EXPLORER	http://www.microsoft.com/ie/logo.asp

Not a site for those with bad eyesight as the writing is so small (a site for sore eyes?). And if Netscape is bad for pestering you with e-mails, Microsoft has raised it to the level of a fine art.

Anti-virus software

This is dealt with in a section of its own (page 15), but there are three big anti-virus software producers (at least) who will offer 30-day or restricted trials of their products. Once you have bought the package, updates (new virus definition files etc) are usually free.

NORTON ANTIVIRUS   http://www.symantec.com/nav/

Symantec's Peter Norton is one of the gurus of PC
optimisation. All of his products are worth at least trying.
Also, this is a nicely organised site that doesn't overdo the
graphics. Get NAV 5.01 or a later version.

DR SOLOMONS   http://www.drsolomon.com/download/

Likewise, Alan Solomons is another PC fix-it king and has an
excellent suite of products, including anti-virus software.

MCAFEE   http://www.mcafee.com/

McAfee's VirusShield is a personal favourite, since it sits
unobtrusively on the desktop and does its job quietly and
competently. Get the latest version and the newest DAT files
(where the anti-virus information sits).

File utilities

WINZIP   http://www.winzip.com

A lot of your downloads will be zipped (compressed) files and
WinZip is the best way to unzip them. Get WinZip 7 and
remember to pay for it later!

ACROBAT READER   http://www.adobe.com/

Adobe invented the Portable Document Format (pdf) file
system, which is a way of delivering text and image documents
such as manuals and information sheets, in a form that the
reader cannot edit or alter. Many downloadable documents
now come as pdfs rather than Word or HTML documents. The
Acrobat Reader is free. Get Version 3.0 or higher, and the site
allows you to specify a nearby host for faster access.

Multimedia

SHOCKWAVE   http://www.macromedia.com/

Many web designers use Macromedia's Shockwave and Flash

to deliver multimedia. The add-ons needed to play such files are available free. Make sure you get the correct versions for your browser. After downloading and installing, return to this site and check out the 'Shocked Site of the Day' to see some examples.

REAL PLAYER   http://www.real.co.uk/

This allows the playback of audio and video within your browser and is well worth having as more and more sites have multimedia components.

QUICKTIME   http://www.apple.com/quicktime/download/index.html

With Quicktime 4, streaming video, sound, music, 3-D and virtual reality can be yours. Remember to choose the PC or Mac version.

Privacy

LUCKMAN'S ANONYMOUS COOKIE   http://www.luckman.com/

When you surf the web, companies may collect information about you without your knowledge (such as your name, phone number, and so on) which will be stored on your computer in a file usually called cookie.txt. Cookies can be created whenever you fill in a questionnaire or a text box, register for a download or order something on-line. When you access a web site, the host can scan your disc and take your cookie information to use (or sell) as they see fit. Luckman's Anonymous Cookie restores your privacy by enabling or disabling all cookies as you see fit. A must! The man deserves a prize.

Every journey starts with a single step. On the web, it's usually a search. Any one of these search engine main pages could be set up as your browsers home page so that it is your first point of contact each time you log on.

ALTAVISTA   http://www.altavista.digital.com/

This is the biggie – probably the fastest and most powerful searcher available. AltaVista was developed by Digital, a major computer company. The massive indexed site database can be a bit cumbersome to search, with its own syntax (AND, OR, NOT etc) but it also has Categories and Specialty Searches to help.

NETSCAPE SEARCH   http://home.netscape.com/home/internet-search.html

When you click the Search button in Netscape, this is where you end up. Powered by Excite (see below) it also allows access to Lycos, Infoseek and other search engines, plus its own Look Smart category lists.

EXCITE   http://www.excite.co.uk/

This takes a directory-driven approach, like Yahoo!, but has the added nicety of being able to personalise itself so that it displays your horoscope, shares, football team results, local weather etc. Using this as your browser home page would present you with personalised information each log-on. As a searcher, it is fast and accurate.

GOTO   http://www.goto.com/

This is what the World Wide Web Worm became and it is disturbingly simple. It started life, the mythology goes, as a napkin sketch of a logo, a search field and a Submit button. No clutter. And it works.

INFOSEEK
http://www.infoseek.com/

This is a true portal, with news, easy links to meaningful subject areas, shopping and community interests all within a well-designed interface.

LYCOS
http://www.lycos.com/

Lycos started as an academic exercise from an American university and it bears those hallmarks. It is extensive (90 per cent web coverage is claimed) and therefore it can be difficult to do narrow searches. However, Lycos has built a network of 'best-of-breed' on-line services for community, chat, e-mail, shopping, web-page building and personalised news. It claims to be the second most visited 'hub' on the web.

YAHOO!
http://www.yahoo.co.uk/

Yahoo! pioneered the 'directory' approach which can help narrow a search down to meaningful areas and also has the advantage of finding UK and Ireland sites only if you so choose.

A OL
http://www.aol.com/netfind/

Intended mainly for those who use America Online as their ISP, this site is nonetheless useful as a general search engine, with relevancy rankings given for each site found – a great help in refining searches.

HOTBOT
http://www.hotbot.com

If HotBot really indexes over six million web sites daily, as is claimed, then it deserves to be the top-ranked search engine. The search options are excellent (e.g. must include, date, location, domain, word stemming) which can deliver very pointed results with one search.

LOOKSMART
http://www.looksmart.co.uk/

This is Netscape's directory-based service with 24,000 categories and sites given 'Best' and 'Worst' ratings and it can also be set as a UK-directed version.

DOGPILE   http://www.dogpile.com

As its name suggests, Dogpile doesn't take itself too seriously and calls itself 'the Friendly Multi-Engine Search Tool'. Essentially, it uses a number of other searchers to pull together a comprehensive search list.

COOL LINKS   http://sunstartechnet.com/cool.html

This is simply a page which links to a number of search engines – SavvySearch, Excite, InfoSeek, WebCrawler, Lycos, AliWeb, DejaNews, MetaCrawler, AltaVista, Yahoo!, Open Text, Archie and Netfind – useful in itself.

TELDIR   http://www.teldir.com/

Telephone Directories on the web – although most search engines have a People Finder option, the ability to look through telephone books is sometimes just what you want. Those which are on-line are accessible from Teldir. These are only as good as their owners make them – for instance, the UK *White Pages* isn't always accurate, up-to-date or complete. British Telecom owns the copyright to UK phone listings.

ASK JEEVES   http://www.askjeeves.com/

Saving the best until almost last, meet Jeeves. This is nothing short of a miracle. You can genuinely ask Jeeves a question like 'Why is grass green?' or 'Why do I never see baby pigeons?' and get a sensible answer, or at least a good place to find out. Compare this with the human-based Allexperts.com http://www.allexperts.com/ in the Reference section (page 64).

ALEXA   http://www.filez.com/alexa.html

Alexa is not a search engine but a free navigation service which adds context to content. It works with your existing browser and has features such as:

- information on who is behind your favourite web site
- site ratings

- recommended links to related sites
- archiving so that if a page or web site is no longer available, Alexa may find a copy eliminating the dreaded '404 Not Found'
- the chance to write your own review
- reference tools from Encyclopaedia Britannica Online and Merriam-Webster's Dictionary and Thesaurus.

There are different downloadable versions for Explorer 4/5 and Netscape. It can be a bit fragile and crash your browser, so be warned.

Like all forms of human endeavour, the web is prone to abuse. It has proved difficult to censor and there are constant arguments as to whether it should be or not (who would do it, for one thing). There are, however, two main ways in which anyone concerned about the nature of material available can filter it to some extent:

1. Set your browser's options to screen out unwanted material. Internet Explorer allows you to modify View, Internet Options, Content: click on the Content Advisor, choose or enter a password and specify which RSAC rating (see below) you are prepared to tolerate. Netscape has Safesurf built in.

2. Acquire one of the censorship packages listed below. Usually they have a month's free trial after which you register and pay. Some have an additional monthly charge.

The Recreational Software Advisory Council (RSAC) was established, with the support of Micropsoft, IBM, Disney and others, to provide ratings for web and internet content and uses the Platform for Internet Content Selection (PICS) infrastructure to provide ratings on sites.

INTERNET WATCH FOUNDATION http://www.internetwatch.org.uk

This UK body was set up in 1996 to monitor dubious and potentially illegal information on the internet and anything reported to the above site or via the hotline (01223 236077) will be taken up with the ISP or host concerned and reported to the police if necessary.

RSAC http://www.rsac.org

This has information on the RSAC, navigation to other pages which allow rating, registration of your web site and reports on relevant topics.

NET NANNY http://www.netnanny.com/

Download the trial or full version Net Nanny, one of the major content filters, from this site. The program filters content, and it can also prevent data from going out onto the web, such as your address, phone and other personal and sensitive information.

| CYBERPATROL | http://www.cyberpatrol.com/ |

The other major filter program can be downloaded from this site, which also contains Route 6-16, a searchable list of links guaranteed safe for children.

| SURFWATCH | http://www1.surfwatch.com/ |

SurfWatch claims to have invented the internet content filtering concept and to be over 90 per cent effective in preventing access to objectionable sites. The 'www1' is not a misprint.

| SAFESURF | http://www.safesurf.com/ |

On the other hand, SafeSurf claims to be the original internet rating system. Netscape Navigator 4.5 comes with built-in support for SafeSurf. Internet Explorer can also be configured to support SafeSurf ratings. SafeSurf is an international parents' organisation formed to protect children, which pioneered the first rating system, and has been at the forefront of fending off proposed government censorship of the web. The 'Kid's Wave' is a safe list of entertainment and education sites.

| PICS | http://www.w3.org/pics/ |

This is the official Platform for Internet Content Selection (PICS) site – very basic layout but a host of links to useful, relevant and often technical material on ratings and filtering.

| CYBERSITTER | http://www.solidoak.com/ |

This is a cheap, reliable filter which sits in the background, blocks disallowed access and maintains a history list. Look out kids – your parents know where you've been!

INTERNET IN A BOX FOR KIDS

http://www.cnet.com/content/reviews/hands/120595/ibox.html

This combines SurfWatch blocking software with a facility to list sites that CompuServe thinks appeals to 8- to 14-year-olds: MTV, Lego, news, sport, FreeZone (articles, comics, chat area, encyclopaedias, dictionaries, and so on) and links to cool sites. There is a monthly and hourly charge to access CompuServe. Click the Cybersitter site (above) for a review.

Two of the three crucial aspects of web page construction are good implementation – which comes down to effective use of HTML – and good design. The third is good content, and that's up to the author. However, there is a great deal of help out there on the first two.

HTML guides

DESIGNING WEB PAGES
http://www.mtsu.edu/mtsu/web/help/design.html

This is a straightforward checklist of things to think about when designing web pages. It is as good a place to start as any.

TIM BERNERS-LEE STYLE GUIDE FOR ONLINE HYPERTEXT
http://www.w3.org/hypertext/www/provider/style/overview.html

For the authoritative word on HTML, who better than the man largely responsible for the web? This is essential reading for anyone serious about web design.

SUN ON THE NET
http://www.sun.com/sun-on-net/uidesign/

Sun Microsystems' User Interface Design is an excellent and comprehensive discussion of what to consider when designing web pages. Another *must* read.

YALE WEB STYLE GUIDE
http://info.med.yale.edu/caim/manual/contents.html

Authoritative, complete and above all large, this guide to creating web pages has sections on interface design in web systems, page design, and performance optimising. The annotated bibliographies provided are comprehensive – if anything, overmuch.

COMPOSING GOOD HTML
http://www.cs.cmu.edu/~tilt/cgh/

This is a useful guide to a number of the more important issues relating to design of web pages.

DOING GOOD HTML
http://www.harold.com/web/goodhtml.shtml

This brief collection of hints and tips is an easy introduction to some of the more important considerations, but will need to supplemented with further reading.

HTML BAD STYLE PAGE
http://www.earth.com/bad-style/

On the other hand... In fact, this site has a lot of sensible advice from the perspective of 'what not to do'. At its most useful, it can be an aide-memoir or checklist when finalising web pages.

TOP TEN WAYS TO IMPROVE YOUR HOME PAGE
http://www.glover.com/

For advice on the use of jpeg and gif files, background images and so on, this uncomplicated guide has a lot to recommend it.

DESIGN TIPS FOR WEB PAGES
http://www.lehigh.edu/~kaf3/guides/design.html

Once you have digested some of the weightier documents given above, this site is a useful short guide to web page design issues. I have a print-out stuck to the wall above my PC. Not that it makes any difference.

DR WILSON'S 12 WEB PAGE DESIGN DECISIONS
http://www.wilsonweb.com/articles/12design.htm

For any business considering implementing a web site, these are some of the major issues to consider. A lot of them are equally suitable for home pages.

ADVICE FOR HTML AUTHORS
http://ugweb.cs.ualberta.ca/~gerald/guild/style.html

The HTML Writers Guild offers sound advice for web designers, and provides links to other useful tools and resources.

AUTHORING HTML DOCUMENTS USING WORD
http://www.anu.edu.au/cnip/authors/tips/word-html.html

Anyone who has tried to convert Word or Rich Text Format

(rtf) documents to HTML will understand the need for software that does it well and intelligently. The site includes one of the best, *rtftohtml*.

WEB PUBLISHING STANDARDS http://www.anu.edu.au/cnip/standards/

Anyone implementing a large web site, such as that of the Australian National University, needs a set of standards for electronic publishing, otherwise the site ends up looking like a jigsaw puzzle.The ANU's comprehensive documents are an excellent resource for anyone considering a similar exercise.

WEB INFORMATION PROVIDER'S HANDBOOK
http://www.ithaca.edu/ip/ip_handbook/index.html

Similarly, Ithaca College produces web publishing guidelines which are full of good, sound practice and excellent advice.

WEBREFERENCE http://www.webreference.com/

This site is a generally useful place to find resources for web authors, designers and programmers. It also contains a list of electronic magazines (e-zines) which are related to the web and provides pointers to many magazines with a short description of each one. This is a good starting point if you are looking for e-zines talking about web publishing and design. Try the search engine – it appears to send the world's longest cookie.

One of the best ways to find good sites is to pick ones thought highly of by others. Hence web awards, a system of recognising and rewarding sites which are well-designed, fast-loading, informative or all three. At least, that's how it all started. Now, some of these are no more than a scam or at least a mutual admiration society based on link exchanges. Admittedly, it is hard to get a site added to the major search engines like Yahoo!, AltaVista or HotBot, so awards emerged as a way to increase traffic. At best, they are excellent navigational aids. At worst, they are just another form of selling you something. How many are there? Read on...

1000 WEB AWARDS   http://members.aol.com/youraward/1000awards/home.html

This is a site of sites. Claiming to access 1,400 award sites in its database, 1000WA lists all kinds of award from the best known and best regarded to the whimsical – have a look at Dancing Finger O' Sarcasm. Awards sites are categorised (Daily, Weekly etc but also, for some reason, Equestrian, Genealogy, Horror and Martial Arts) and also listed alphabetically. This site benefits from a minimum of graphics and programming wizardry to keep it accessible to many browsers.

SUPER CYBER SITE AWARDS   http://www.snowcrest.net/casson/awardsites.html

'This is not a reciprocal link program' Super Cyber Site proudly announces. It is a simple to use and clear, uncluttered site in its own right.

THE WEB AWARDS   http://www.thewebawards.com/

This award site is so well thought-out, clear and well categorised that it would make a good home page for your browser. Full marks and deserving of an award in its own right.

HIGH FIVE   http://www.highfive.com/core/index.html

Hi5 grants monthly awards for excellence in web site design, conception, execution and content. For a good guide to what constitutes clear, informative, visually attractive sites, there is no better place to start than here.

Apart from writing good HTML codes, the other crucial aspect of web site construction is page design. This section lists useful resources for designers, including tyros. Refer also to the section on backgrounds, images and animations (page 18).

THE WWW VIRTUAL LIBRARY: DESIGN   http://www.dh.umu.se/vlib.html

This is one of the major guides to design resources on the web which, if used selectively, is an excellent place to start gathering information on the design and construction of web pages.

ARTS WIRE PUBLIC WEB PAGE: MAP   http://www.tmn.com/0h/Artswire/www/awmap.html

This web site has links to a number of graphic art sites including arts organisations with web pages which are worth visiting. This is a good way to get design ideas.

TRANSPARENT AND INTERLACED GIFS   http://www.nctweb.com/nct/software/transgif.html

Gif files can be confusing. The basic rule is not to mix non-transparent and interlaced gifs, but there is more to it than that. This tutorial addresses the differences between transparent and other gif files and deals with interlacing.

INFOSEEK GUIDE: CLIP ART
http://guide-p.infoseek.com/DB?tis=1328&tid=532&db=101&sv=N1&lk=noframes&col=WW

There are many places to get clipart sites on the web and this site lists the best ones.

PLANET EARTH HOME PAGE   http://www.nosc.mil/planet_earth/images.html

This is a very good links listing of art, flags, icons, images, maps and postcard clipart on the web. Some are copyright free.

NETSCAPE COLOR PALETTE   http://www.onr.com/user/lights/netcol.html

It is not always easy to know which colours will work best in

Netscape without dithering. This page includes an extremely useful gif file with the 216 (not 256) colours used in Netscape.

RGB HEX TRIPLET COLOR CHART   http://www.phoenix.net/~jacobson/rgb.html

Converting colour decimals to hexadecimal values and *vice versa* can be a pain. This site provides a guide to background and text colours for use in web sites, with their associated values.

This Section is divided into meaningful groupings for ease of use.

Tax

INLAND REVENUE   http://www.inlandrevenue.gov.uk/

Now and again, someone you would absolutely not expect gets it absolutely right. The tax site is a delight. Hector the Inspector (the cute pinstriped character from the TV adverts) is your guide to self-assessment, with all the forms and guides on-line and downloadable. It even starts 'Good afternoon'. Lovely. And I know at least one otherwise sensible and boring chartered accountant (sorry, Jim) who gets great fun out of the Beat The Taxman screen saver. Either the Inland Revenue has finally hired someone with a sense of humour or the web designers deserve a medal. They appear not to deserve a mention, which is a pity.

Personal finance

CONSUMER INFO   http://www.consumerinfo.com/index.html

How's your credit rating? If you don't know, lots of other people do, including anyone you apply to for finance, insurance, credit cards etc. Sign up for a free 30-day trial, and you receive a credit report. If you continue, the CreditCheck Monitoring Service will send you information on your credit. You will know everything credit checkers know. Comforting, isn't it?

QUICKEN FINANCIAL NETWORK   http://www.quicken.co.uk/

This is an excellent personal finance site by Quicken (producers of personal finance software and now owned by Microsoft) and the *Financial Times*. Specially interesting features are the interactive insurance, mortgage, tax and savings sections, and the tax calculator. Apparently my income tax bill will be £150.82 less this year. Worth knowing.

MONEYWORLD
http://www.moneyworld.co.uk/

This is one of the best introductions to personal finance available anywhere. There are guides to important aspects like mortgages and pensions, a good news service, a large directory of financial institutions, share prices and excellent consumer information. The inevitable advertisers offer discounts and there are links to the web sites of most UK finance houses. It looks businesslike and is very easy to use but hard to get lost in.

MONEYEXTRA
http://www.moneyextra.co.uk/

This site is tied somewhat to Microsoft's program, MS Money, although it is not essential to use the software to get something out of this site. Its best feature is the comparison tables for the cheapest or best loans, credit cards, deposit accounts, mortgages etc. It also contains good guides to money matters. Registration is necessary.

NATIONAL SAVINGS
http://www.nationalsavings.co.uk/

Think you might have a Premium Bond that came up trumps but you didn't know about it? Search Ernie on-line to find out. This is a good example of an attractive web site used to front a dull but worthy subject, including the tax rules on the bewildering variety of National Savings products, ISAs and how to invest.

Property and mortgages

INTERNET PROPERTY FINDER
http://www.propertyfinder.co.uk/

There are numerous on-line property sites, but IPF is one of the most comprehensive. It covers properties to buy or rent plus farms and commercial property. A number of the large, national estate agents list properties here, including General Accident, Halifax and Royal & SunAlliance. The service is free to users – the agents pay – and the search forms are easy to use. It also has good, simple advice on mortgages.

MORTGAGE BUREAU (U.K.)   http://www.mb-uk.co.uk/html/home.html

This is one of the least nosey of on-line mortgage enquiry sites, which doesn't require you to divulge every last detail about your personal circumstances before accepting information on which to send an e-mail quote. If you are comparing prices for lending, this site, with its access to a variety of lenders, would give you a benchmark at least.

Shares

INTERACTIVE INVESTOR   http://www.iii.co.uk/

This is aimed more at the serious investor and can search company share prices, independent financial advisers and the performance of investment funds. A lot of it is reserved for registered users but a surprising amount of information is free, including some extremely readable guides to investment. There are links to related sites dealing with ISAs, offshore investments and the like. The Net Community facilities and forums are interesting.

CHARLES SCHWAB   http://www.schwab-worldwide.com/worldwide/europe/sterling/

This on-line share dealing service is frighteningly straightforward and allows the sort of electronic buy-and-sell capability that brings out the Nick Leeson in all of us. Their base site http://www.schwab.com/ is an excellent resource for investment news, real-time investment discussions and investing tips and research.

QUOTE.COM   http://www.quote.com

How are your shares doing? Quote can tell you. There is an interesting 'symbol lookup' facility (since nobody can remember what their favourite share's symbol is), plus company snapshots, an excellent series of charts and the opportunity to build a 'My Portfolio' query which will report on your own batch of holdings. Simple to use yet extensive in its reach, Quote is the web at its best.

FIDELITY INVESTMENTS   http://www.fidelity.co.uk/

This is the UK arm of http://www.fidelity.com which was instrumental in forcing the acceptance of virtual signature technology, which allows you to (for instance) open accounts via the internet and move money around. There are also facilities to review investments and look at fund performance. There is far more going on behind this site than at first appears.

Insurance

SCREENTRADE   http://www.screentrade.co.uk/

It doesn't take a genius to figure out that if replacing insurance and pensions salesmen with call centre operators cuts costs and makes for cheaper products, then taking the whole insurance brokering service on-line is the next logical step. There is no guarantee that the prices quoted here are always the lowest, but what is it worth not to be on the end of one of those interminable phone calls while sorting out your car cover? This is on-line shopping at its best, for services you would be buying anyway.

LEGAL & GENERAL   http://www.landg.com/

This insurance company was among the first to take the web seriously and has won a number of prestigious awards for handing control back to the user. Track your mortgage payments, take out medical insurance and find out where your nearest approved hospital is. The site is bright, attractive and easy to use. Note the .com address, part of a trend by UK companies to look more international by avoiding the .co.uk ending, which is reckoned to have a 'provincial' feel to it and could scare off the lucrative US market.

Banking

WELLS FARGO BANK   http://www.wellsfargo.com

I do confess – if I lived in the USA I would bank with Wells

Fargo. Not only do they give you a chequebook with picture of stage coaches all over it, they have by far the most exciting web site of any bank. There are stories from Wells Fargo's history, an interactive Wells Fargo museum with photos and paintings of the wild west, and every day a true story from the company's colourful past. This is an excellent resource for teachers, students and Louis Lamour fans everywhere. It makes you want to put on a mask and go hold up a train. Yee-Hah!

BANKING REVIEW   http://www.bankreview.org.uk/

You may not be fascinated by the Review of Banking Services in the UK, but this independent investigation of banking is looking at innovation, competition and efficiency in the industry and how well it serves the needs of business, consumers and the UK economy. What is interesting is that all the working documents and the final report (due at the end of 1999) will be available on this site, which will also take responses during the consultation process. This is open government at its best. The web site itself is sober, august and understated, as befits the subject, and designers The Reading Room are to be congratulated.

General

WSJ: MONEY AND INVESTING UPDATE   http://update.wsj.com/

What can you say – it's the *Wall Street Journal*. There is a subscription option, but a lot of information on this busy and business-like web site is free.

GET READY FOR THE EURO   http://www.euro.gov.uk/

What my American friends persist in calling the EuroDollar is with us. What it means for UK businesses is less than clear. The UK government has put up this web site which contains information for UK businesses adjusting to the introduction of the Euro in 1999. The site is straightforward and informative – essentially a series of FAQs and answers, plus an up-to-date list of conversion rates.

COMPANIES IN BANKING AND FINANCE   http://www.mrweb.co.uk/dotcom/fina-co.htm

It may not seem like much, but this simple page of links has the web site of your bank, building society, credit card company, merchant bank and accountant. A useful, helpful web resource. Thanks.

ANTI-ROM   http://www.antirom.com/

This interactive design agency bills their Anti-Rom site as a 'non linear journey'. It mostly consists of shockwave items. Put your sound on and move your mouse within some of the pictures. A plus point is that all the files are fairly small so do not take ages to load. It's either a design experiment or it's art. Or maybe it's just all a game. Whichever, some of these are extremely clever and represent what's possible at the edges of web technology.

FETISH   http://www2.gol.com/users/zapkdarc/fetish.html

Despite the name, it's actually a showcase for weird Japanese design. If you like station-cleaning robots, a toothbrush that ionises away bad breath and an alarm that fits in your ear so you never miss a train stop (a Japanese obsession, apparently) or over-boil an egg (Japanese housewives have been known to commit suicide over that!) this is the site for you.

MAIL ART   http://www.club.innet.lu/~year0891/mailart.html

On the other hand, in Luxembourg they are more concerned with the artistic possibilities of postcards, stamps, envelopes, artistamps (worth finding out) and the SEND A CAN project. Cheer the man up and send him a tin. Good site for pig lovers, too.

DENNETT'S DREAM   http://www.cgrg.ohio-state.edu/~mlewis/gallery/smtitle.html

Not a museum, not an art gallery really, but weird! Needs the Cosmo Player plug-in for Netscape.

SURVIVAL RESEARCH LABORATORIES   http://www.srl.org/

SRL and Mark Pauline started the whole Robot Wars trend. This site is a record of his machines, shows, ritualised combat exercises between devices designed for destruction and what they themselves call 'The Unexpected Destruction of Elaborately Engineered Artifacts'.

URBAN DIARY   http://gertrude.art.uiuc.edu/ludgate/the/place/urban_diary/intro.html

This site 'chronicles the life and thoughts of an anonymous urban citizen' in its own words. Anyone looking to have their prejudices reinforced as to the real value of art schools would do well to start here. UIUC is well known for its avante-garde on-line art projects. This one purports to be the 'found' pages from a journal of an artist, with interesting use of clickable image maps and some stunning visuals.

GENE ART   http://www.albedo.co.uk/geneart/index.cfm

This interactive art page allows the creation of modernistic art works based on circles, ellipses, squares and rectangles which then evolve. Select a composition as the 'parent' and watch the next generations emerge. You could be the next Modigliani.

PI   http://www.pithemovie.com

This is the official web site for the Darren Aronofsky film. One of the more interesting 'arts' films of recent years now has one of the more interesting accompanying 'arts' web presences.

KAPELICA GALLERY   http://www.kapelica.org/

The kids at the Students Organisation of the University of Ljublijana are defining the cyber-arts of tomorrow. There is nothing else like it on the web.

We really should get out more. Shall we go to the theatre, download a clip from the latest Rolling Stones DVD, book a ticket for the opera or find out what's on the telly? Better still, let's find out where *Casablanca* is playing this week and see if there's a curry house nearby. At least we won't waste another evening web-surfing!

BBC ONLINE   http://www.bbc.co.uk/

This is a truly integrated site, which goes beyond listings to include news, weather, education and everything you would expect from Auntie, including a Jobs List with on-line application forms for all the aspiring media moguls out there.

ITV   http://www.itv.co.uk/

The ITV site offers daily listings, TV region selection and links to specific sub-sites for all your favourites (*Coronation Street, Home and Away, Blind Date*).

MTV   http://www.mtv.com/

Anyone into popular music will want to access this on-line magazine from the premier TV music channel. Apart from the obvious listings and MTV-related news, this site also has a useful alphabetical list of bands. Only the latest and greatest are there – no Beatles, for example! Mind you, ZZ Top made it.

SCIFI   http://www.scifi.com/

The on-line guide to everything on the SciFi channel will not need selling to science fiction enthusiasts in terms of content. But it has the added bonus of being well designed and can be personalised to your own preferences (such as which SciFi TV channel you watch). There is a UK feed for faster browsing.

STAR TREK CONTINUUM   http://www.startrek.com

This is the official home of *Star Trek* on the web, so it has everything that you might expect, including what the fans most want – a newsgroup so they have a place to grumble. Other non-official sites offer more options (endless discussions on the detail of Klingon uniforms, for instance) but this is The Real Thing. It is also not resource-hungry, unlike sites which are laden with jpeg files that take forever to load. More *Star Trek* sites are listed in the dedicated section (page 173).

TV GUIDE ONLINE   http://www.tvguide.com/

Previously called TV Gen, this is the web site for those of us whose TVs don't have on-screen channel listings. The expected daily channel guides are there, plus the usual celebrity articles and news. There is also a good video database with playable clips.

FILM.COM   http://www.film.com/

This excellent and comprehensive web site for film buffs offers news, stories, reviews and film clips, plus the chance to buy movie memorabilia. It is also the host of the *Watch It* awards, featuring a short film playable in its entirety on your desktop PC. This requires the latest RealPlayer G2 software, which is downloadable free.

FILM FINDER   http://www.yell.co.uk/yell/ff/home.html

What's on at the flicks? Here's the place to find out. It genuinely had the latest information on films showing in my small town. Plus info on the films and the phone number of the cinema so I could check. This site is an alliance of *Yellow Pages* and the Press Associataion. Then it listed the restaurant/pub/taxi near to the cinema by using a *Yellow Pages* search (one of each category my personal favourites). It works!

ALOUD.COM   http://www.aloud.com/

This UK-based On-line Ticket Service, Event Guide and Venue Directory is exactly what it says – buy a ticket for just about anything, just about anywhere. Really.

UK THEATRE WEB   http://www.uktw.co.uk/listings.html

Caliban (Combined Arts Listings in Britain and Northern Ireland) has a large, if not a complete, listing of events in UK theatres. Check here for your next outing.

RSC   http://www.rsc.org.uk/

The Royal Shakespeare Company's site is gorgeous. Although there is no on-line ticket sales facility at the time of writing, it is planned. In the meantime, forward schedule with play synopsis and cast list is worthwhile and the education site is wonderful.

There are more entertainment-linked sites in Travel Resources (page 165).

Two of the three greatest pleasures in life are eating in and eating out. Both are catered for, with variable success, by a large number of web sites, many of which are no more than dressed-up opportunities to buy things or inadequate guides to places no one would want to eat at anyway. But there are some good guides to food in general and places to enjoy it, plus some excellent commercial sites offering genuine gustatory bargains. And for those of us who simply enjoy reading about food and wine we may never actually taste, or who have a deep desire to find the ideal coulis to serve with marinated haggis, there is somewhere on the web which has the answer. Savoury sites abound, and those below are merely a starter.

ELECTRONIC GOURMET GUIDE   http://www.foodwine.com/

Now folded in with The Global Gourmet, this Californian site is a rich mine of practical and easily-digested (!) advice and information on the whole business of food and wine. A tasty web site.

BOOKS-FOR-COOKS   http://www.books-for-cooks.com/

Want a cookbook? This is the place. A specialist bookstore-cum-web site, even if you never buy a book there is an immense amount of information for food lovers here, including recipes. Very American, but that in itself means a diversity of ethnic cookery information.

WINE & DINE RESTAURANTS   http://www.winedine.co.uk/thedines.html

I seriously doubt that there is a more comprehensive or worthwhile guide to restaurants anywhere on the web. It is not extensive, but each eaterie is rolled around in the mouth and savoured by seasoned wine and food writers. The site is spoilt by poor execution and looks like somebody finished off the HTML code after a rather good lunch. However, it's one to write on the back of a menu and take home. See also Wine & Dine e-zine (below).

EUROMENU   http://www.euromenu.com/

This site provides a search of restaurants in France, Spain, Italy, Ireland, Scotland, England and Wales by a long list of cuisine types – including, helpfully, non-smoking and Family Pub. It is simple, effective and well-designed and helps narrow down the search for a good night out. There is no Cajun in Cardiff but there is a Brasserie in Belfast. The nice touch is that it displays the menu.

DINE-OUT!   http://www.dine-out.co.uk/

Described as 'Britain's Ultimate Restaurant Guide' it may well be once they get their database problems sorted out. The idea is a good one – search for a restaurant anywhere in the UK by name, town, type of food etc but also by postcode or STD code. In theory, therefore, 0121 will produce a list of restaurants in Birmingham. It does, but unfortunately includes other restaurants nowhere near. Even if there is a Bombay Palace in Hereford, why does it give the address of one in Glasgow? I suspect the database picks the first one of the same name. If Dine-out! can fix this, it will be a truly useful site. There is also a facility to add restaurants you like. A nice idea in need of some tweaking.

KIDS & CO.   http://www.intelligent-era.co.uk/kids%26co/

Worried about what the kids eat and whether all the junk food is damaging? This UK childcare site is for anyone who is involved in looking after children, or looking for childcare. It contains useful information on children's nutrition and foods which justifies its inclusion here. There are suggested dishes for toddlers and fun recipes for children to make plus creative ideas for things to make. A caring site.

SAINSBURYS ONLINE   http://www.sainsburys.co.uk/orderline/main.asp

One day I will bite the bullet and have all my groceries delivered from an on-line order rather than walk the 400 metres to Tesco. If I do, I may well choose Sainsbury. It is well-designed, fast and easy to navigate. The catch? They don't deliver to my area. Is it raining outside?

INTERACTIVE FOOD FINDER   http://www.olen.com/food/

Would you like to know the nutritional information for more than 1,000 items sold in fast-food restaurants? Search here by calories, fat cholesterol and sodium. Clearly the Minnesota Attorney General's Office, on whose work this site is based, is a true, if unlikely, subversive. A fun idea, with a useful, healthy purpose. If I mentioned the take-away chain with the highest percentage of fat in the burgers, I would be sued. You can check for yourself.

MIMI'S CYBER KITCHEN   http://www.cyber-kitchen.com/

This may well be the largest and most complete food and cookery site on the web. There are links to hundreds of other food-related sites, plus recipes.

WINE & DINE E-ZINE   http://www.winedine.co.uk/

This is a delightful site – idiosyncratic, opinionated, quirky and guaranteed to appeal to the guzzler in us all. It also has some amazing things for sale that say a lot about the web author, Tony le Ray (a cure for snoring, for one). He justifies two entries in this section (see Wine & Dine Restaurants).

DAD'S IN THE KITCHEN   http://www.dinersgrapevine.com/dik/index.html

Oh, yes! A web site dedicated to the idea that fathers could cook too, if they did but try. Nice idea, funny graphics and tidy execution.

THE GLOBAL GASTRONOMER   http://www.cs.yale.edu/~hupfer/global/gastronomer.html

Select a region from the clickable map and escuriate your way through the world's cooking. A great site, nicely executed and fun. Foods of Antarctica deserves a special mention.

SOAR   http://soar.berkeley.edu/recipes/

Need the correct recipe for Gesztenye Kremleves (cream of chestnut soup) but can't lay your hands on it? Start with the Searchable On-line Archive of Recipes and find anything you want. The site is also indexed by major eating opportunities (breakfasts, appetisers, Christmas etc) and by ethnic groups. A great resource for the kitchen wizard.

THE CYBERSPACE WINE MAP http://www.winebiz.com/

This is a 'trade' site about wine, originating in Napa Valley, California, home of what Americans call 'domestic' wines. It is a treasure chest of information about wines and their enjoyment. Pour a glass and dip in.

THE WINE PAGE http://www.speakeasy.org/~winepage/

This is a real hidden site – nobody knows it exists and there's no way to get there from the www.speakeasy.org main site that I can see. But it is just packed with wine information. A full-bodied sub-site with a lingering afterglow. In particular, look at http://www.speakeasy.org/~winepage/cellar/codedfaq.html#9

WINE LINKS http://www.speakeasy.org/~winepage/winelink.html

This is a site of links to other web sites about wine. Much of the web consists of nothing more than pointers to other sites. However, this site offers content as well, with a commentary on each site chosen. Someone has done a great deal of homework here, so profit from it.

Other sites

The following sites are recommended for specialist tastes:

CHATEAU ONLINE http://www.chateauonline.co.uk/

---

and

WINE CELLAR UK http://www.winecellar.co.uk/

On-line wine sellers with good information.

CULINARY CAFÉ http://www.yumyum.com/

The Microsoft cooking site.

CULINARY CONNECTION   http://www.culinary.com//

Good, basic advice in an approachable manner.

DIGESTIVE DISORDERS   http://www.digestivedisorders.org.uk/

Flatulence, food poisoning and other light reading before your dinner.

DINER'S DIGEST   http://match.cuisinenet.com/digest/custom/etiquette/tips_pitfalls.shtml

Table manners and etiquette. Sit up at table!

FOOD AND DRINK   http://www.bbc.co.uk/foodanddrink/

The BBC's excellent TV programme is now on an excellent web site, with 150 recipes, and a wine-tasting course from Clarke and Goolden.

GASTRONOMER   http://www.gastronomer.com/

Despite the high-sounding name, this is basic, practical advice for those new to the kitchen, and good for herbs and spices.

I LOVE CHEESE   http://www.ilovecheese.com/

Three guesses what this American Dairy Association site is about, but it does have good cheese recipes and cheese profiles, plus a news section, Cheese Bytes.

MEALS FOR YOU   http://www.mealsforyou.com/

Healthy eating meal plans and recipes in this huge and well-designed site. Plan your meal and it writes your shopping list.

VEGETARIAN RESOURCE GROUP   http://www.vrg.org/

Beyond the nut cutlet to sound advice on nutrition recipes and travel for vegetarians.

VIRTUAL CHOCOLATE   http://virtualchocolate.com/

E-mail pictures of chocolate to fellow addicts.

WINE BRATS http://www.wine.brats.org/

Tipplers jargon demystified.

YUMYUM http://www.yumyum.com/

Cooking queries answered by Gidget.

PORTMAN GROUP http://www.portman-group.org.uk/

Sobering thought time. This drinks industry body exists to encourage 'sensible' drinking, and their 10th Anniversary web site allows us all to calculate how many tots will result in good health or a rapid decline. The Proof of Age scheme and the Quiz are nice features.

Everything said about virtual museums in the relevant section (page 139) applies just as well to galleries. Some places which call themselves museums are actually, or also, galleries and vice-versa, so there are one or two duplicate links. The destinations below are provided without any commentary, since all the chosen examples combine good design and navigation with excellent content and are all worth visiting to see how it can be done.

VAN GOGH'S VAN GOGHS	http://www.artmuseum.com/
THE INTERNET PUBLIC LIBRARY	http://ipl.sils.umich.edu/
SHAKESPEARE HOMEPAGE	http://the-tech.mit.edu/shakespeare/works.html
VIRTUALMUSEUM	http://www.cgrg.ohio-state.edu/~mlewis/gallery/gallery.html
THE WHITNEY MUSEUM OF AMERICAN ART	
	http://www.echonyc.com/~whitney/
WEBMUSEUM:BIENVENUE!	http://www.emf.net/louvre/
THE FINE ARTS MUSEUMS OF SAN FRANCISCO	
	http://www.island.com/famsf/famsf_welcome.html
THE METROPOLITAN MUSEUM OF ART	
	http://www.metmuseum.org/htmlfile/opening/enter.html
PARIS PAGES MUSEE DU LOUVRE	http://www.paris.org/musees/louvre/
THE WORLD-WIDE WEB VIRTUAL LIBRARY	
	http://www.w3.org/hypertext/datasources/bysubject/overview2.html

---

One of the best features of the web is its unlimited capacity for things one person finds fascinating and very few others have any interest in at all. But if only a handful of people share an obsession with fifth-century Athenian pottery, why should they not have a medium by which to share their passion? On the other hand, there are many mass-market collection-based hobbies which absolutely depend on having access to databases, catalogues and up-to-the-minute information. The web caters superbly for all these and this section can do no more than scratch the surface.

Antiques

SOTHEBY'S   http://www.sothebys.com/

This outstanding site features the expected know-how and collectors advice as well as interactive adventures. There are also excellent sections on auctions, auction results and schedules, collecting in general, a gallery guide, glossary, on-line catalogues, a search service, information on tax, trusts and estates, a good history section and more besides. The design is also well-conceived and the navigation is helpful.

Autographs

CELEBRITY ADDRESSES   http://www.springrose.com/celebrity/main.html

Want Arnold Schwarzenegger's address? Here it is. This site has an A–Z listing of the famous so autograph hunters can write to them. Alternatively, the postal and e-mail addresses of British celebrities are at Neil & Kevin's British Celebrity Address Archive (http://wkweb5.cableinet.co.uk/passfield/). This site is also part of the Autograph Ring, so there are many other sites to explore, including some with autograph galleries. Some unscrupulous people have been known to print these and pass them off as real. Imagine such a thing!

Beer and beer collecting

PUB PARAPHERNALIA   http://www.pub-paraphernalia.com/

It takes an American to put up the quintessential site about the English pub. Pub Paraphernalia is a site dedicated to gifts and souvenirs of the British Pub – ashtrays, mirrors, bar towels, pub signs, figurines and yards of ale. This is a sales site for serious collectors. For a more amateur and more fun example, look at George's Tegestology Page (http://stoopidsoftware.com/beer/info.html#what) and find out what the term 'tegestology' means plus a short history of beer mats with trade or sell possibilities. Someone in the UK with a fondness for pubs and an e-mail address could make a lot of money collecting and selling drip mats bulk to Americans.

NICHOLSON'S WALL OF BEER   http://www.wallofbeer.com/

This site is a testament to one man's thirst as it is an exhibition of beers he has actually drunk and therefore 'collected'. Introduce yourself at the beer board, post a link, or just admire Nicholson's crusade to drink every known bottled beverage.

Books

ANTIQBOOK   http://www.antiqbook.com/index.html

This Dutch site (with an English version) has an excellent set of on-line catalogues, searchable databases and information about auctions, exhibitions, book fairs and markets, booksellers' catalogues and directories, plus a free book search service. The bibliographical information has a good link list to pages with useful information and the antiquarian book resources are among the best on the web. A useful feature is Valuta which converts guilders into other currencies.

BOOKSEARCH UK   http://www.booksearchuk.co.uk/

This well-established book search service will find out-of-print books for the public, and for universities, libraries, companies, government departments and book dealers who use the service to find their customers. A search for up to four books is free for new enquirers. The quoted price for the book includes commission and postage. The Booksearch Request routine is straightforward and fast.

Clocks and watches

WATCH IT!   http://www.xs4all.nl/~rkeulen/watch/

Watch It! is a Dutch monthly e-zine for clock and watch collectors, with facts and figures, articles, classifieds and access to back issues. Alternatively, The Owners' Guide (http://www.dircon.co.uk/lockes/table.htm) is a thoroughly useful site full of information about pocket watches, wristwatches, clocks and barometers. There are clear sections on how to wind plus faults and maintenance information. But the real site for this is the Index of Workshop Hints and Tips (http://www.bhi.co.uk/hints/index.htm) – said to be the world's most comprehensive collection of on-line horological repair tips, it is maintained by the British Horological Institute. And who better?

Coins and numismatics

AG AND S GILLIS   http://ourworld.compuserve.com/homepages/andy_gillis/

This nicely organised site specialises in Anglo-Saxon coinage. The well-indexed catalogue has images and ordering information. A good links site is Collector Link (http://www.collector-link.com/coins/). Search the database of web sites and newsgroups for coins, currency, medals, proofs, tokens and stock and bond certificates. UK Coin Heritage (http://www.erols.com/annet/CLIENTS/UKCH/UKCH-index.html and do watch the capitalisation) has complete year sets of modern British coins, plus sets featuring individual kings and queens. This is worth a visit even if you don't intend to buy.

Comics

COLLECTING COMICS http://www.collecting-comics.com/museum/default.asp

This is the best place for collectors. The Comic Book Museum showcases the greatest comic books from hard-to-find examples of the 1940s and 1950s to current favourites. Visitors can add their own comics to the database and buy/sell/trade by e-mail. Oh, why did I give all mine away? Admirers of gaudy heroic iconography will find much to admire (and download) at:

THE DARK KNIGHT http://www.darkknight.ca/dknight.html

with its excellent interactives, while aspiring comics writers will pore over:

DC COMICS SUBMISSION GUIDELINES http://www.dccomics.com/guides/guides.htm

Philately

STAMP COLLECTING http://www.geocities.com/heartland/2769/

This falls into the Enthiastic Amateur category of web sites, but means well and has some good images. On the other hand, there's Wardrop.

WARDROP'S PHILATELY ONLINE http://www.wardrop.co.uk/

This aims to be a one-stop site for access to all information on stamps and stamp collecting. Full of interest in its own right, not least for its on-line auctions and the search engine which delves into the Wardrop links, this is a great starting place for extensive and well-researched links elsewhere. If you need Romanian Counties Postal Codes, here they are!

Toys

DR. TOY'S GUIDE http://www.drtoy.com/

Although intended primarily as a site for information on the best toys and educational products, there is a great deal here for the serious toy collector, including articles, resources and links to other toy sites.

There are more cars in the UK than houses, so motoring is obviously popular. The web offers everything from buy-and-sell to technical information on esoteric marques. There are also excellent sites on road safety and car insurance, special number plates and new car reviews, Formula 1 and go-karts. Turn the key, press the pedal and zoom away! It's safer than actually driving.

AUTOLOCATE   http://autolocate.uk.msn.com/

This site allows the car-seeking surfer to locate new and used cars from dealers in the UK. There are two search modes – one which allows specification of make, model, price and distance from your postcode, and the second a wizard which guides you through the same process. It appears to access over 500 dealers.

AUTOEXPRESS   http://www.autoexpress.co.uk/

Yes, it looks like a car dashboard, which provides surprisingly good navigation. 'First with car news and reviews' it claims, and it is certainly comprehensive and detailed.

BBC TOP GEAR   http://www.topgear.beeb.com/

In another of the BBC's excellent TV-to-magazine-to-web exercises, Jeremy Clarkson and his chums get to drive the hairiest cars and bikes and enthuse about them. Apart from excellent and relevant links, the site has a daily news section, a car chase feature and fantasy Formula 1.

BRITISHCAR   http://www.britishcar.com/

Not all Americans drive Cadillacs. Some have the sense to stick to classic British sports cars. Don't let the US focus put you off – affiliated to *British Car Magazine* this excellent site has a library section with articles and information on different models and their makers, details of the 150 or so British car events held in America every year and links to owners' web pages, mostly Triumph.

CYBERDRIVE   http://www.cyberdrive.co.uk/index.html

Driving test coming up soon? The Virtual Driving Theory Test might help. The Stationery Office (publishers of the Highway Code) and the Driving Standards Agency have collaborated on this site which allows you to improve your knowledge before taking the actual Theory Test. Alternatively, take a test right away using your credit card. There is a database of over 600 questions, five Theory Test papers and an index of TSO publications to order to help you pass your test.

CLASSIC CARS WORLD   http://www.classiccarsworld.co.uk/

Old banger or sought-after classic? This web site, based on the famous mag of similar name, will show you how to tell the difference and even how to convert one into the other or where to buy that special model, plus information on its running cost, coachwork, engine, transmission and the rest. The auction news and car ads sections show likely purchase opportunities. The events calendar is good and the Classic Chat forum is where to find the enthusiasts. A well-balanced, authoritative site, even for the casual browser.

LEARNER DRIVERS UK   http://www.learners.co.uk/

Don't be put off by the amateurish, cartoony design – there is pure gold in here. Apart from a directory of driving schools by area there is information on off-road training for under-17s, sections on driving test theory and practical tests, hints on passing, advanced driving, resources and links for learners and a free interactive theory test. Good content, but in need of a professional redesign.

NEW CAR NET   http://www.new-car-net.co.uk/

This is an independent guide to new cars in the UK, with images, information, performance figures, insurance quotations and pictures on every make and model. Check here before you buy.

SPORTS CAR SPECIAL   http://www.pil.net/~mowogmg/home.html

MG fanatics start here. Fans of the MGA, MGB, Midget and

other variants can join the virtual car club meeting each week, enjoy and contribute to the image gallery or technical info section. The best feature of the site is its largely annotated links to other UK car sites but with an MG bias. Where it scores is in the enthusiasm which oozes from every pixel and hyperlink.

SISA CLASSIC CAR INSURANCE — http://www.sisa.co.uk/moto8b.htm

The Special Insurance Schemes Agency offers insurance on almost any category of risk – not just motor but also health, marine, household and others. A lengthy, detailed form elicits a quotation by e-mail and cover is arranged directly with no telephone calls or correspondence.

CAR REGISTRATION AT DVLA — http://www.dvla-som.co.uk/index.html

For that special number for that special car, start at the Driver and Vehicle Licensing Agency. This excellent, well-organised and informative site deals with not only the nuts and bolts of vehicle licencing, but also historical trivia, the acquisition of 'cherished', classic and select registration numbers (B1 MBO went for £18,000 and B10 PSY for £4,500), plus details of registration number auctions. A neat gearstick navigation aid is an added nicety. To search for the availability of chosen numbers, look at the Cherished Numbers Dealers Association site (http://www.reg.co.uk/) and for the whole intricate business of licence plate collecting start with the cutely named PL8S (http://www.pl8s.com/index.htm).

UNLEADED PETROL — http://www.environment.detr.gov.uk/unleaded/index.htm

By January 2000 leaded petrol will have been phased out. Do you need unleaded or additives? Does your engine need modifying? Is yours a classic car? This site may be useful – but for particular cars, go to http://www.autodata.ltd.uk/ for the *Unleaded Petrol Information Manual*. Autodata sells a book listing all engines. The AA and RAC offer information (AA tel: 0990 500 600, RAC tel: 0990 722 722). Crypton, the engine tuning people, keeps a list of UK vehicle manufacturers on the web at http://www.cryptontechnology.com/manufac.htm. Your car's maker may have information.

On last checking, there were over 2,000 museum web sites and that's probably a vast underestimate. About 50 are considered to be any good. Interestingly, the Scottish Museums Council could not tell me which museums in Scotland had a web site. Some do, but none is included in this selection. The list is a subjective one, but uses the following criteria:

- Good design.

- Pushing the technology to its limits.

- Forgetting the physical structure of the museum or gallery and using cyberspace intelligently.

- Improving and updating all the time.

- Somebody obviously cares.

- All good museums and galleries are not about objects but about the relationships between objects and a narrative. In other words, they tell a story, whether it's evolution, taxonomy or the progression of a culture. The same must be true of virtual museums.

The seven sins of museum web sites

1. **Glass-case-and-card**. Often, a web site is no more than a digitisation of the guidebook, in which case you might as well have the guidebook.

2. **Floor plans.** It makes sense to show the floor plan of the museum, as this is useful to know if preparing for a visit. However, to arrange the virtual museum as a carbon-copy of the physical museum is to miss the opportunity to relate objects, recreate a narrative and provide meaning rather than a linear experience. Why take away physical walls to replace them with electronic ones?

3. **Passive viewing**. If all I can do is stare at the screen and see a progression of pictures, an opportunity has been missed. If, however, I can be guided, interact with the objects, look at them from different angles, interrogate ever-deeper databases and ask for on-line assistance – the virtual equivalent of the old-style museum guide who knew endless funny stories about each and every artefact – I will have a more fulfilling experience and I will be in that museum like a shot next time I visit that town.

4. **Techo-naivety.** The software exists to allow almost any form of arrangement, interaction, navigation and information retrieval we can think of. Yet most virtual museums are two-dimensional and the navigation linear. The possibilities are not pushed to the limit.

5. **Lack of standardisation**. There is a rather confused jumble of storage and retrieval methodologies extant, although large-scale projects like SCRAN 2000 in Scotland, AHIP in America and a plethora of G7 and European initiatives will force standards on museums and prevent anyone getting into a VHS/Betamax/Phillips blind alley.

6. **Promotion.** In most cases the web page is used as no more than an electronic hand-bill and mail-order exercise for the gift shop. If I don't have a worthwhile experience in your web site, I won't buy your T-shirt.

7. **Low bandwidth.** Usually, the web site has been constructed grudgingly by a recent graduate or interested staff member, in his or her spare time, on a budget that wouldn't pay the light bill and via a server than can't cope. This rules out in-line movies, 3-D animations, direct interactivity and other experiences that would add value to the exercise.

The links provided below are to good museum sites which have remembered most or all of the above and created a worthwhile virtual space to get absorbed in.

General sources

VLMP http://www.comlab.ox.ac.uk/archive/other/museums

The World Wide Web Virtual Library museums pages by J.P. Bowen are a good place to start searches. Alternatively, another good jumping-off point is http://www.w3.org/hypertext/DataSources/bySubject/Overview2.html. Look under Humanities for Museums.

EXAMPLES OF VIRTUAL MUSEUMS

http://www.pacificrim.net/~mckenzie/jan96/museums.html

A selective but reasonable collection.

MCN LIST   http://world.std.com/~mcn

The Museum Computer Network maintains a hotlist of over 500 museums on the web.

Nine virtual museums

SCRAN   http://www.scran.ac.uk/

The Scottish Cultural Resource Access Network is, in its own words, 'A parcel o' multimeja for a nation'. This is a Millennium Project to build a networked multimedia resource base for the study, teaching and appreciation of history and material culture in Scotland. SCRAN intends to have 1.5 million records on-line, 100,000 multimedia objects and 100 CD-ROMs.

PALAEOLITHIC PAINTED CAVE   http://www.culture.fr/culture/arcnat/chauvet/en/gvpda-d.htm

Brilliant images and excellent text from the recently discovered cave at Vallon–Pont-d'Arc. Apart from this 'virtual museum' the caves are 'off limits' to protect the fragile cave paintings, so this is the best opportunity to see them.

VATICAN   http://www.christusrex.org/www1/vaticano/0-musei.html

The Vatican's *Christus Rex et Redemptor Mundi* is one of the top 100 sites on the web, according to *PC Magazine*, and certainly one of the best virtual art museums.

WEBMUSEUM   http://sunsite.doc.ic.ac.uk/wm/

The original! Formerly the WebLouvre, this is at the UK mirror site above and also at others in the USA and elsewhere. It is more generally available via
http://www.yahoo.com/Art/Museums/Le_Louvre/

FMNH   http://www.fmnh.org./

The Field Museum of Natural History, Chicago, is a good example of making the best use of new web technology. Check out the running triceratops!

IMSS http://galileo.imss.firenze.it/museo/4/index.html

The Institute and Museum of the History of Science of Florence, Italy, is a personal favourite, and Galileo would have liked it too.

NHM http://www.nhm.ac.uk/museum/tempexhib/vrml/index.html

See the virtual reality fossils at The Natural History Museum through a project called Scalable Interactive Continuous Media server design and Application (SICMA) supported by the EU Advanced Communications Technologies and Services programme. Be aware, the VR takes an age to download. The next phase of the project will allow home owners in Belgium of all places to access the virtual museum via a cable television network. This is also a good place to find a link to VRML software.

CULTURAL MAP OF GREECE http://www.culture.gr/2/21/maps/hellas.html

This site is incomplete but getting there, and a model of how to use a web site to whet the cultural/travelling appetite.

EXPO http://sunsite.unc.edu/expo/

This is a good example of how *not* to make the best use of the web, although a bold effort to make an ordinary experience look cyber-cute.

It's your art

TAX-EXEMPTED ART http://www.cto.eds.co.uk/

This Inland Revenue site is included purely in the interests of causing unrest. There is a little-known but much exploited tax loophole which allows owners of works of art, antique furniture etc to avoid the payment of inheritance tax if they are displayed to the public. It is absolutely the right of any UK taxpayer to get reasonable access to these on the day of their choosing or, if not convenient, between 10am and 4pm on any one of at least three weekdays or two Saturdays or Sundays in the four weeks following a request, and do not be put off by talk of proof of identity, letters of reference or waiting lists. The Register of Conditionally Exempt Works of Art does not list owners or exact locations of the art works, but does have a search engine organised by region and type of art work and gives details of agents (usually solicitors) through whom viewing can be arranged.

The ability to play decent quality audio is relatively new to home computing and is the result of improved hardware and some rather clever web technologies. Without going into detail on MPs, the difference between .wav and .au files and the relative merits of Real Player and Media Player, suffice it to say that there is a great deal of good sound out there readily available. If you want to hear a track from the latest release, listen to a radio station you could never receive over the airwaves or find a sound clip to embellish your desktop, it's all there for the asking. If phone calls were free, web could easily replace radio.

CD NOW http://www.cdnow.com/

This is absolutely the place to buy CDs, the aural equivalent of Amazon. Be careful of incurring import tax and VAT (see page 80). It also has reviews, sound clips and a personalisation feature so that you can browse for the music it knows you like.

MUSIC WEBB http://www.webb.com/musicwebb/

Isn't Webb Cliff Richard's real name? In fact Webb is a New York outfit and their music sub-site is a good place for music fandom.

THE INTERNET DJ http://www.internetdj.com/

Whether you like alternative, dance, jazz, oldies, rock, hip-hop or techno the DJ will play your request in Real Audio. There are also channels, music links and the opportunity to customise a CD on-line and have it sent to you.

SOUNDRESOURCE.NET http://www.soundresource.net/

This is one of the largest WAV and MP3 archives on the web. SoundResource holds over 2,000 sound clips from films, cartoons and television shows as well as other media. This is the place to get clips like Homer Simpson saying 32 Dohs in 15 seconds. Right click to save to your disc, remembering at all times to respect others' copyright! Other good sites are

MP3.com (http://www.mp3.com) which has free resources and MPEG.org (http://www.mpeg.org) with good links to other free sites.

IUMA
http://www.iuma.com/iuma/index_graphic.html

The Internet Underground Music Archive claims to feature the music of over 3,000 independent musicians. It also has a number of very nice touches, not least the retro-50s design. For those with a slow connection there is a cut-down version (IUMA-Lite). There is a training package on how to manipulate downloadable and streaming sound for the web, with a CD-ROM of software utilities and song samples. An on-line music store has 350,000 CDs, news, reviews and over 200,000 audio samples! There is also a 'radio station' for on-line broadcasting of 100 songs while you surf.

ON LINE GUITAR ARCHIVE
http://www.olga.net/

How did he play that? OLGA is the place to search for your favorite song or favourite band's guitar tablatures and chords. As the site itelf points out, this is for study and private practice purposes, of course, rather than any idea of performing. Dear me, no.

WORLD WIDE ROCK AND ROLL
http://www.geocities.com/motorcity/3227/rock.html

This page has a wide variety of useful features – for instance, downloadable rock videos, links to favourite bands, a visit to the Rock 'n Roll Hall of Fame and other resources for the afficionado of the heads-down mindless boogie. Kerrannggg!

MIDI WEB RESOURCES
http://midibiz.w1.com/websites/websoft.htm

Windows comes with a restricted range of playable MIDI tunes. Anyone with a desire to explore the area of sound creation further should start here There are various downloadable midi programs for music writing and replaying with descriptions of their functions, plus sound samples.

NOTEWORTHY COMPOSER http://www.keyscreen.com/KeyScreen(s)7/noteworthy.htm

---

An unashamed plug here – there is no better program for composing, writing and printing music than Noteworthy Composer. Screenshot is a good place to download the time-limited version. You will fall in love with it.

SUN RECORDS http://www.sunrecords.com/

For the Elvis, Orbison and Cash fans, there is nowhere else to go. Choose from over 5,000 classic recordings and hear the music before buying.

Lonely? Never go out? Stare at your PC all the time? One obvious use of the web is to find like-minded people and see if there's a soul-mate out there. A vast array of agencies has sprung up to service this need, and so has the apparently unending supply of Russian female graduates and Ugandan princesses to marry.

SELECTIVE SINGLES   http://www.infobios.co.uk/ssingles/

This is a UK-based Dating and Introduction Service. Basically you complete an Attitude Profile then e-mail it (or print it off and post or fax it) and you will be snowed under by e-mails from compatible people, with any luck. If you like pink and pastels, you'll love the design of this site.

HANDIDATE   http://ourworld.compuserve.com/homepages/conrad_packwood/

This introduction agency specialises in people with disabilities. Set up by Conrad Packwood, who has cerebral palsy, Handidate was launched in 1987 on BBC TV. This is a worthy cause and an excellent use of the web aimed at people who will make the most out of its accessibility. However, it is not really on-line as you send in your name and postal address and an information pack and application form come by mail.

CUPID'S NETWORK   http://www.cupidnet.com/

This site brings together Nationwide sites (meaning the USA), International sites (an extensive list that I counted to be over 400 links and which includes Russian Romance, Marriage Tours and the wonderfully named SingleJew.com), Phone and Chat Lines, Singles Events (in America), Religious Sites, Singles Travel, Singles Literature and a Bookstore. If what you want is *El Consultorio Sentimental de la Dra. Corazones* (free love advice in Spanish) this is the site for you. Apparently I'm compatible with three women in Alabama who'd love to meet me. Plane fare?

DATEMAKER   http://www.datemaker.co.uk/

Now this is a really clever site that makes excellent if rather cheeky use of the web's database integration possibilities. If you searched for, say, singles OR dating OR introduction AND Berkshire, you would get a page which would simply take you (always) to the home page. An example would be 'Click here for Love in Co Fermanagh' which seems like a reasonable request. Once you register you receive an ID etc plus the chance to answer 60 questions and some essays (do it off-line!). The service appears to be free, so I tried it. Within three days I had had eight replies. I answered the first one and three weeks later we were married and her mother made me Duke of Kent. Honest.

FRIENDFINDER   http://friendfinder.com/

After the usual questions the site allows you to set up preferences. It is fast with a good, framed design and easy navigation. You will have to sign up before searching for likely companions and be a Silver or Gold member (which costs). Mind you, the Adult FriendFinder is worth it! Once registered, you can browse listings (with photos if supplied) and, Praise the Lord, it even recognises Scotland and Wales as distinct from United Kingdom in some of the drop-down lists. It does, however, keep trying to pair me with people in Chester. What's wrong with Chester that nobody speaks to each other?

ONE & ONLY   http://www.one-and-only.com/

Here you can browse ads, see personal information (culled from submitted profiles), place your own ad then sign up for the Agent of Love which will e-mail you with new ads – all for free. How are these people making any money? It is also possible to generate a listing with photos, which appears to contain the entire female population of the Ukraine.

Sport is popular. Fantasising about sport is even more popular. Slumping out thinking about sport is universal. The web is an ideal medium for the last two of these.

SOCCERNET   http://www.soccernet.com/

Another Cool Site and Award for Soccer Excellence winner, this site is top of its premier league – good, simple design, lots of relevant content, excellent galleries of action images and easy navigation. The Analysis section gives betting odds and stats (goals, results and injuries). Soccer information, live scores, results, tables, fixtures, daily news, club and player biographies, match analysis and trivia are all here. You'll be over the moon.

INTERNATIONAL FOOTBALL HALL OF FAME

http://www.sporting-life.com/soccer/halloffame/

The USA has had Baseball and Basketball Halls of Fame since the1930s, so in 1997, England decided to honour the worlds best footballers. Linked to a planned interactive museum of football in Manchester, this site allows visitors to vote for their favourite players (retired for at least three years). Of the first batch, it is no surprise that Pele was top.

HALF DECENT WEBSITE   http://www.wsc.co.uk/wsc/

The self-deprecating title of this site, associated with the fans magazine *When Saturday Comes*, puts the fun back on the terraces. Check out the match reports from the spectator's point of view (contribute your own), a guide to the best football-crazy pubs and 'Pele's poetry'.

ROUGH & READY BASKETBALL   http://www.ukhoops.com/

The Rough and Ready tournament takes place every May in Brixton. This site has background, this year's game schedule and some video clips and images, plus information on young players and good links to other hoop sites.

SCRUM http://www.scrum.com/

Scrum.com has won a Cool Award, Cool Site of the Day and a nomination for the 1998 Yell Web Award. This is one of the best rugby sites on the web, with an updated results service for all UK, Europe and international matches. There are news updates, tables, fixtures, squad and club information and a weekly profile of top players who are then added to the growing archive of Who's Who in Rugby. For live audio of the Five Nations games, interviews with players and live reports before and after kick-off, Netshow is required. Alternatively, at weekends there are audio commentaries, views and interviews. 'In the Bar' has a postcards service, bulletin board and live question sessions with rugby folk. The weekly quiz is also good. A great site and a true service to a great sport.

GYM PARTNER SEARCH http://www.users.dircon.co.uk/~muscles/gym.htm

This is a service for males looking for someone to train with, based on statistics, exercise regime, preferred gym and training times. Even if you avoid this aspect of the site, there are training tips, how to set up a home gym, charts, an introduction to the whole business of working out and pictures of the muscle-bound to inspire you.

WIMBLEDON http://www.wimbledon.org/

This 'official' site has historical information, player profiles, statistics, video and audio interviews and a Shockwave tennis match plus details of the upcoming Championships, with a ticket-booking service promised.

WATERSKIING IN CYBERSPACE http://www.waterski-uk.com/

Those who know the fakie from the revert and the switchstance and those who have no idea of the difference between cable-skiing and kneeboarding or wakeboarding and slalom will take an interest in this informative (if visually dull) site. Technical hints and historical facts abound. One for the converted, but newcomers will also find a lot of interest to them.

SKY SPORTS HOMEPAGE
http://www.sky.co.uk/sports/center/index.htm

With all the latest scores and stories from the cable channel, this sports news web site is extremely good for the most popular televised sports (football, boxing, tennis, rugby, cricket, golf and the NFL). The text is in very small type and the use of visuals makes for slow loading, but it's all there.

UK SPORTSZINE
http://www.sportszine.co.uk/

This site covers the usual sports, but also those that Sky Sports (above) ignores, such as scubadiving, sailing, Formula 1 racing and sky diving. There are no features, but it is a great place for links to other sites for information on fixtures, events, travel, training programmes and publications, even if it is marred by adverts that open up in new browser windows. However, you can close these. The most popular feature, predictably, is the monthly Swimsuit section.

CRICINFO
http://cricinfo.cse.ogi.edu/

This is a truly impressive database-driven site, with everything the cricket lover needs to know. Register first at http://cricinfo.cse.ogi.edu/PLEASE_REGISTER.html (not the link they give you, and it isn't obvious) and get a wealth of data on the current series, plus live coverage, results, news articles, a shop and access to the immense database of pictures, players, statistics and grounds. The Archive and Interviews sections are good and the links to clubs and societies extensive.

SKI MAPS
http://www.skimaps.com/

There is far more than just skiing resort maps here – news, travel information, features, snow reports, video and a shop plus a search engine and links to over 400 resorts world-wide.

TENNIS COUNTRY
http://www.tenniscountry.com/

This site calls itself The Total Tennis Resource, and it may be right. Easy to navigate with clickable images, Tennis Country works like a club, with members from over 50 countries. The latest tennis news and tournament results, chat forums with fans and players, a free tennis lesson, links to exotic resorts for tennis holidays and a Players' Lounge with audio and video on-line interviews and contests are all there. Registration required.

GOLF AT ST ANDREWS   http://www.standrews.co.uk/

Where else? Actually a tourist information site, and a good one, this site has excellent links to other golf courses as well as golfing history, hotels, places to visit and things to buy in Fife. Note: the author of this book has no hidden agenda in attracting visitors to his native county and spending money!

THE 19TH HOLE   http://19thhole.com/

More complete and well-designed, this site combines the on-line magazine approach with the required detail and trivia that golfers adore. On the Practice Tee features the mental side of the game. Golf Fitness deals with exercise and nutrition. In the Lounge has a message board facility. The Duffers features golf's funniest family as they travel the fairways and bunkers of life. Golf art, a good photography section, scorecard collections, golf-related books, videos and software plus links to literally hundreds of golf-related web sites round off this perfect alternative to three frustrating hours in the rain.

FLY FISHING IN THE UK   http://www.fishandfly.co.uk/

Is it a sport? Never mind. Whether you fish for trout, salmon, grayling, pike or saltwater fish, Fish and Fly will be of interest. The monthly editorial from Jon Beer (*Trout and Salmon*), news and reviews and a directory of fly-fishing products and services make this a great source of on-line information for the angler. The best feature is the message board and fly fishing update – anglers can contribute news about local fishing conditions. There is also information on and links to organisations such as the Wild Trout Society, the Anglers' Conservation Association and the Salmon & Trout Association.

The web is an unparalleled educational and informational resource and has the potential to present a vast array of complex knowledge in a codified manner. Anything you would ever want to know is somewhere on the web and, fortunately (but not surprisingly), a lot of people and bodies with an interest in science also have a desire to publicise it. Science sites are among the best presented and worthiest sites available. Most of us will never visit Jupiter, the ocean bed or the inside of an amoeba, but we can all share a sense of what these would be like. The web really started as a way for scientists to share information with each other, but now we can all benefit.

Archaeology and paleontology

VIRTUAL ARCHEOLOGY   http://www.sgi.com/features/1997/archeology/

Silicon Graphics' site has virtual reality archaeology. Download the appropriate browser plug-in (if you don't have it) and tour the ancient sites.

ARCHNET   http://archnet.uconn.edu/

This virtual library for archaeology has many links to the sites of archaeological projects and to archaeological and palaeontological museums. The site itself is packed with relevant images and information.

Biology

BIOCHEMISTRY CHIME SAMPLES   http://www.mdli.co.uk/support/chime/cool.htm

MDL Worldwide Services provides a complete biochemistry textbook making good use of the possibilities inherent in a 3-D viewer. There are other graphical science resources here, too.

NATIONAL AGRICULTURAL LIBRARY   http://www.nal.usda.gov/speccoll/

This is an excellent site for rare plants, botanical prints, forest insects, plant pests and diseases and other aspects of botany and agriculture.

Chemistry

WWW VIRTUAL LIBRARY http://www.chem.ucla.edu/chempointers.html

The chemistry section of the WWWVL (see page 64) is an unparalleled source for all things chemical, for amateurs, public, students and professional scientists alike.

CENTER FOR SCIENTIFIC COMPUTING http://www.csc.fi:80/lul/chem/graphics.html

CSC hosts a chemical art gallery full of images of electrons, atoms, molecules, proteins and polymers. Science as art has never been so well represented as here. Some of the images may require special plug-ins or viewers.

Earth sciences

NASA EARTH SCIENCE http://pao.gsfc.nasa.gov/gsfc/earth/pictures/earthpic.htm

Goodness knows what NASA spends on film developing every year, but it is to their eternal credit that they make so much of it available. This page holds the latest images of Earth taken from various research platforms in space.

ISBISTER http://www.isbister.com/worldtime/index.html

If you need to know the exact time anywhere on Earth, Isbister (makers of time management software) have a free site which will tell you to the second. This is great for synchronising your Windows clock.

Energy

NREL http://www.nrel.gov/data/pix

This collection of renewable energy and environmental technology photographs from the National Renewable Energy Laboratory is a terrific resource for any project on the environment. The links in the site are extensive and well-researched.

Engineering

THE NATIONAL INSTITUTE OF STANDARDS AND TECHNOLOGY
http://www.nist.gov/public_affairs/gallery/galindex.htm

The NIST's image gallery includes high technology equipment and developments and pictures of its labs. Use the links to get to other engineering resources.

Entomology

COLORADO STATE UNIVERSITY   http://www.colostate.edu/depts/entomology/images.html

Given that there are over one million species of parasitic wasps alone, there is no chance that any entomological image collection will be complete. But the departments of entomology at CSU and at Iowa State (below) have a good try. CSU hosts an extensive collection featuring images of insects, arthropods and their relatives. The indexing is clear, even for those untrained in taxonomy. The movies of various insects are interesting.

IOWA STATE UNIVERSITY   http://www.ent.iastate.edu/imagegallery/

For information on and pictures of common pests (ticks, fleas, flies, mosquitos etc), start here. There is an excellent index of online insect images.

General

EUREKALERT   http://www.eurekalert.org

The American Association for the Advancement of Science (AAAS) has an excellent up-to-date science news site which is one of the best places to track what's going on in the world of science and technology.

NEW SCIENTIST   http://www.newscientist.com/ps/

This excellent science magazine is covered more fully in the Newsstand section (page 48). It is the best first resource for news, features, interesting links and background information.

NATURE — http://www.nature.com/

Register (free) and you have access to the world's most authoritative science news resource. This will allow searches, browsing of the tables of contents and first paragraphs and a free weekly e-mail summary of *Nature*'s contents. Subscribing brings more benefits, including linking from references to abstracts in the ISI and Medline databases. There are also science job adverts and a link to an international grants register for fund-seekers.

SCIENCE MAGAZINE — http://www.sciencemag.org/

Browse, search and read current articles or the archive of America's prime science publication. The most useful feature is the Hot Picks – the best of science, pre-chosen, with links. Like *Nature* (above), there is an e-mail updating service. *Science* is aimed at professionals, but ScienceNow (http://www.sciencenow.org/) is its on-line public service, including a good historical and archive section, Science Then.

NOBEL PRIZE ARCHIVE — http://nobelprizes.com/nobel/nobel.html

Who won what, when, and for what? What did Einstein actually do? Relevant information, literature and other resources are all here. And for more on Albert himself, browse Albert Einstein Online (http://www.firstmonday.dk/issues/issue2_2/friedman/#dep1)

NPR SCIENCE FRIDAY KIDS CONNECTION — http://www.npr.org/programs/sfkids/

National Public Radio is the only US equivalent of our own Radio Four. Much of its scientific radio output suitable for school-age children is available in a sound archive, which features a lot of the world's greatest science journalist, Joe Palca, who now owes me a large meal!

SCIENCEDIRECT — http://www.sciencedirect.com/

Elsevier's site offers access to more than 1,000 scientific, technical and medical journals and publications. There is also an excellent set of links to other science resources, mainly aimed at working research scientists, but worthwhile for a general scan, too.

THE SMITHSONIAN   http://www.si.edu/activity/start.htm

Take a day off, a deep breath and a flask of coffee, then plunge into this vast and incredible site covering all aspects of the Smithsonians collections. I counted more than 1,000 pages. Start at the Photographic Services Data Base (http://www.si.edu/cgi-bin/image_archive.pl) which has over 900 gif files on all subjects – Air and Space, Science, Nature, Technology, History and People-Places.

Marine biology

NATIONAL OCEANIC AND ATMOSPHERIC ADMINISTRATION

http://www.graysreef.nos.noaa.gov/pictures.html

NOAA's Gray's Reef National Marine Sanctuary has a superb collection of underwater images, vertebrates and invertebrates. Just like a trip in a glass-bottomed boat.

Mathematics

GEOMETRY MODELLERS   http://www.sdsc.edu/vrml/gmmodelers.html#ez3dvrmlauthor

---

See the VRML section (page 33) for more information, then explore this site for tools to make gemoetrical shapes in 2-D and 3-D.

Medicine

MEDLINE   http://www.nlm.nih.gov

The US National Library of Medicine's Medline is a wonderful portal to all aspects of medicine. It includes a search facility, puckishly titled 'Grateful Med' which accesses a number of huge databases including the wonderful Spaceline, a collection of information on space medicine and the effects of low gravity on human physiology. PubMed has access to 9 million medical citations including complete genome sequences and Medline Plus contains consumer health information. This is the most complete medical reference source available anywhere.

SLEEP HOME PAGES — http://www.sleephomepages.org/

Everything you ever wanted to know about sleep from UCLA, including an on-line textbook on sleep, research updates, bibliographies, links to sleep labs and clinics and far more.

VISIBLE HUMAN PROJECT

http://www.nlm.nih.gov/research/visible/visible_human.html#viewers

The Visible Human is an ambitious project to render a body as a data set. This site provides links to various visualisation projects using this.
For the gynaecologist in all of us, the Stanford Visible Female site (http://summit.stanford.edu/RESEARCH/StanfordVisibleFemale/images.html) has 3-D images of a cryopreserved female pelvis, should you need such a thing.

Physics

LAWRENCE LIVERMORE LABORATORY — http://www.llnl.gov/graphics/images_clips.html

Science sees things we don't, by using special imaging techniques. The scientific visualisation site has pictures of such esoteric concepts as flow volumes, textured splats, line bundles, spot noise and unstructured volume data texture rendering.

VISUAL MEDIA SOURCES — http://www-visualmedia.fnal.gov/vms_site/v_photographs.html

This is a searchable index of images taken at Fermilab, but none downloadable. For more extensive information, use their links to other physics sites.

CERN — http://wwwas.cern.ch/openday/pressoffice/index.html

The European Laboratory for Particle Physics is the world's largest research centre. The web site offers a vast range of downloadable nuclear physics images and links to other relevant information.

PPARC   http://www.pparc.ac.uk/freebies/pixbank.html

The UK Particle Physics and Astronomy Research Council has
a good collection of physics images, including an excellent
simulation of the Infrared Space Observatory (ISO) in orbit
around Earth.

PHYSICS NEWS GRAPHICS   http://www.aip.org/physnews/graphics

The American Institute of Physics maintains an archive of
images on physics-related topics. They also host the Emilio
Segre Visual Archives (http://www.aip.org/history/esva), a collection
of photographs and biographies of physicists past and present.

Weather and atmospherics

NCAR   http://www.mmm.ucar.edu/

The National Center for Atmospheric Research has a wealth of
information on Earth's atmosphere and interesting visuals.
Particularly good is the water vapour imagery from the GOES-
8 satellite (http://www.mmm.ucar.edu/pm/satellite/small_water_loop.html)
and the more general gallery of satellite images
(http://www.mmm.ucar.edu/pm/satellite/image_gallery.html) plus links to
satellite images of the Earth's weather patterns. At the Radar
Image Gallery (http://www6.etl.noaa.gov/pdj/gallery.html) NOAA
Environmental Technology Laboratory has a good set of radar-
derived images such as clouds, storms, atoms and gravity
waves.

Women in science

WITI   http://www.witi.com/cgi-bin/check.cgi

Anyone with an interest in women's issues in science should
start here at Women In Technology International. There are
on-line magazines, news, information on women in science
and technology jobs, forums, chat places and events calendars.

Zoology

THE NATIONAL ZOO   http://www.si.edu/organiza/museums/zoo/

Apart from the predictable, but extensive and high quality, photographs of mammals, birds, reptiles, amphibians, and invertebrates, there are live video feeds, on-line lectures and an audio tour of the zoo. Since you may never visit it in person, visit it via the web.

Just plain silly

GEORGE GOBLE   http://ghg.ECN.purdue.edu/

What do systems engineers do in their spare time? Wonder no longer – look at George's site and find out how to light a barbecue with liquid oxygen. Wait until it loads . . . this is serious stuff.

Space deserves its own section, distinct from science. Interest in astronomy and cosmology are at an all-time high and there are many sites packed with information and excellent graphics. Refer also to the education section (page 54), where there are some space-related links to more interactive and educational sites.

PLANETARY PHOTOJOURNAL
http://photojournal.jpl.nasa.gov/

This is a collection of many of the best images from NASA's planetary exploration programme, indexed by planet and exploration vehicle. Most are available in gif or jpeg format. Plus there is lots of information about each of the planets. Check out Saturn's rings and moons.

SHOEMAKER-LEVY
http://www.jpl.nasa.gov/sl9/images.html

Remember the comet (Shoemaker-Levy) that hit Jupiter in July 1994? Want to see a few hundred photos from 27 observatories world-wide? This is the place! This site can be slow (or busy) but the images are also at the wonderful 9 Image Archive (http://nssdc.gsfc.nasa.gov/sl9/comet_images.html).

NASA
http://www.hq.nasa.gov/office/pao/library/photo.html

NASA has compiled a large photo gallery of stills, including images of the solar system, the Earth and its oceans, flight vehicles, robotics, aeronautical and space flight equipment, and mission patches. A video gallery (http://www.hq.nasa.gov/office/pao/Library/video.html) includes footage shot from space vehicles; satellite views of hurricanes and monsoons; and live video from NASA Television. Then go to http://www.hq.nasa.gov/office/pao/History/Timeline/apollo13chron.html to find out whether one of the Astronauts on Apollo 13 really did say, 'Houston, we have a problem here.' This is the transcript of the communications the day of the accident.

SIR-C/X-SAR PROJECT
http://www.jpl.nasa.gov/radar/sircxsar/

This US-German-Italian joint initiative provides space radar images useful to fields as disparate as archaeology and climatology.

SEAWIFS PROJECT   http://seawifs.gsfc.nasa.gov/seawifs/images/subregion.html

Create your own custom-designed satellite images for any part of the world.

NINE PLANETS   http://seds.lpl.arizona.edu/billa/tnp/

Bill Arnett's wonderful site shows the planets and major moons in the solar system. Rich with still images, movies and sounds, this feels like a real space voyage. There is also an index of on-line images of the solar system (http://seds.lpl.arizona.edu/billa/nineplanets/picturelist.html)

NRAO   http://orangutan.cv.nrao.edu/images/astro/

The National Observatory site gives access to radio astronomy images plus general astronomical pictures including stars, galaxies and comets.

SOLAR   http://solar.sec.noaa.gov/solar_images/imageindex.cgi

The Space Environment Center keeps an eye on the sun and has a solar images collection of information gathered every day. Likewise, the Solar Data Analysis Center (http://umbra.gsfc.nasa.gov/images/latest.html) maintains a gallery of sun images.

CLEMENTINE   http://www.nrl.navy.mil/clementine/

This site has an excellent range of images and animations of the moon and earth from the Clementine spacecraft as well as an on-line catalogue of the exhibit of Clementine imagery at the National Academy of Sciences.

NSSDC   http://nssdc.gsfc.nasa.gov/photo_gallery/photogallery.html

The National Space Science Data Center's well-indexed photo gallery presents images of the planets, spacecrafts, asteroids, comets, galaxies, globular clusters, and more, gathered by sources such as the Galileo space probe and the Hubble Space Telescope.

STSI   http://oposite.stsci.edu/

The Space Telescope Science Institute's Office of Public
Outreach maintains 'a photo gallery of the universe' which
features the Hubble Space Telescope's most spectacular
images. STSI also maintains a collection of visualisations,
movies, and animations produced by the Astronomy
Visualisation Laboratory. The page also provides a detailed
explanation of what the the Hubble Space Telescope's images
really look like in space and how they are produced. Some
seriously large mpeg files (often 6 MB or more) are worth
downloading. The multimedia show 'Tour the Cosmos' is
excellent. It requires RealAudio and NetShow, downloadable
from the site.

MESSIER   http://seds.lpl.arizona.edu/messier/objects.html

This simple but resource-rich deep space objects page has
information and images of over 100 nebulae, clusters and
galaxies and a numerically sorted list of the Messier objects.

TURFGRASS IN SPACE   http://www.cas.psu.edu/docs/casdept/agronomy/sts90.htm

Golf and grass have made it into outer space – together!. This
site is a homage to turfgrass, lunar bunker shots and the
future of the low-gravity 6-iron. There are also good links to
other space and golfing sites.

So you've decided to visit Peru and need to fly out on Wednesday, catch a bus to the airport, hire a car in Lima, find a hotel and book a guide for your three-month trek through the Andes, having got the necessary vaccinations and visas, and return via EuroDisney. Best of luck. With the web, you won't spend the rest of your life sitting in a travel agent's office surrounded by incormprehensible brochures. Given the ready availability of information and on-line booking systems on the web, it's hard to see how high street tour operator shops stay in business. The day may soon come when they can't afford to.

BUS AND COACH UK   http://nationalexpress.co.uk/

This site goes one further than Railtrack's (below) by taking all the necessary details then allowing on-line booking. There are also special offers, day trips and discount schemes. A simple and effective site that delivers exactly what you expect.

CHEAP FLIGHTS   http://www.cheapflights.co.uk/

This may well be the best source for travel bargains from the UK, and you don't even have to register. It takes you to a selection of agents with flights to the places you indicate, which saves searching the pages of other agents and airlines. Special deals, last-minute bookings plus car and hotel reservation are available – a gem of a site and easy to use.

RAILTRACK   http://www.railtrack.co.uk/

This is exactly what the web is best at – making sense of complex information stored on a database and presenting it simply. No more long calls to busy and uninformed booking agents – just work out where you start from, where you finish, whether you want to go direct or the pretty way and your departure or arrival time and the site will show you the best trains around the indicated times. There is no facility to book tickets, but print out a copy of the schedule and take it to the station – it should cut your booking time in half at least. The design is simple and effective, but I do wish they would get the antique station clock to show the right time.

Initial research for this book indicated that travel was one of the most popular reasons for searching the web. Therefore, this section is extensive. The previous section (page 164) deals with flight, coach and train timetables and booking.

ALL COUNTRIES OF THE WORLD
http://www.inweh.unu.edu/unuinweh/mapdatabase/countries%20of%20the%20world.htm

This is just what it says – links to each country, organised by the United Nations University in Tokyo. But it is fairly unselective and some of the targets are of poor quality or not quite the best. Why would they have chosen http://www.britain.co.uk/ (reviewed below), which is very good but hardly official, over the UK government site of the Tourist Board? Still, if you need to find out quickly about where they mine phosphates in Nuaru, do start here.

AMTRAK   http://www.amtrak.com/

The best part of this site and an absolute vindication of its existence are the scenic route maps which explore some of the most spectacular parts of America. The downloadable maps and timetables (Adobe Acrobat format) are something Railtrack should investigate. The linked booking and accommodation databases are easy to use. The 'frequently asked questions for first-time rail travellers' says more about America than anything. The whole site has a 1960s feel that is very comfy.

AUTO EUROPE   http://www.autoeurope.com/index.shtml

Want to hire a car anywhere in Europe? Then find hotels and travel information for your visits along the way? Auto Europe has a straightforward booking and enquiry form, with no need to give credit card details until actually making a reservation and no cancellation fees. This is a very useful site for the foot-loose traveller.

BRITANNIA
http://britannia.com/

This is an absolutely huge site, encyclopaedic in its scope, containing everything about Britain (see page 61 for a description of its history section). Constructed in the USA and registered in Delaware (which is a tax dodge), the site has mostly UK contributers and is a superb place to start for anyone interested in Britain, its history, institutions, tourist attractions and lots more. Despite the US origins, it is supremely useful for Brits too.

CITY.NET
http://www.city.net/

This is Excite's travel search engine and it has a wealth of information beyond basic destination information, including a Find the Lowest Fare facility that only works for US cities of departure. Shame really.

DISNEYTHEME PARK AND RESORT SITES
http://www.mcs.net/~werner/links.html

This unofficial Disney Parks site contains all the links to all Disney sites, official or otherwise. It's a lot of information in one place and a good place to begin any exploration of the world of Walt.

EURO METRO
http://ourworld.compuserve.com/homepages/robert_sch/euromet.htm

This is a truly useful site, albeit specialised – maps of every underground, metro and subway system. It is fronted up by a clickable map based on a clever idea, the whole world represented as if it were a subway map. Within each city's metro map is other information about the place itself and links to other useful information. Definitely worth a look.

FODOR'S TRAVEL ONLINE
http://www.fodors.com

Fodor's Guides have a justified reputation for being detailed and useful. If anything, the web site is even more so. Apart from the expected features, there is a facility to generate an itinerary based on destination, chosen price range, travel plans etc. It then gives you what is basically a battle plan for your holiday. Impressive!

TRAVEL ADVICE AND WARNINGS   http://193.114.50.10/travel/countryadvice.asp

Who's going to know about the ins and outs of any country and whether it's safe to travel there, if not our very own Foreign and Commonwealth Office? Ah yes, the ones who pooh-poohed the very idea of a war in Bosnia. Still, they do have an extremely comprehensive database of information on each of the world's states. There is also visa information, consular help and other useful advice including our Key Foreign Policy Issues.

HEALTH ADVICE FOR TRAVELLERS   http://www.doh.gov.uk/hat/emerg.htm

This is another official government site, and a good one at that. Where else could you find out whether your trip to Ouagadougou will require vaccinations for dengue, Rocky Mountain spotted fever or cholera, and which malaria tablets to take to which country? There is also a wealth of local information that will be useful to anyone planning a trip to out of the way places. Excellent, straightforward site.

HOTEL GUIDE TO BRITAIN   http://www.britain.co.uk/

Find and book accommodation in London, York, Bath, Edinburgh and 700 hotels in the rest of the UK. The site contains information about heritage attractions, historic houses, and castles, museums and national parks. It also uses clickable maps cleverly to locate your destination.

HOW FAR IS IT?   http://www.indo.com/distance/

This is a great idea – select your starting point and destination and get the distance, plus a map from the Xerox Palo Alto Research Center. Then zoom in to see more and more detail. Simple and useful.

LANDINGS   http://www.landings.com/aviation.html

One for real flying freaks, Landings has everything you ever need to know about aircraft, airports and aviation in general. This is an absolute labour of love by Drive Inc. and Dr Günther Eichhorn of the Smithsonian Astrophysical Observatory. The claimed 13,000,000 visitors is not surprising for such a rich, deep site. Apart from pilot information, there are links to, for example, all major airports. A nice coda: the official Edinburgh Airport site (http://www.baa.co.uk/edinburg/navigaed.html) was down or unreachable, but Joe Curry's unofficial site (http://www.users.zetnet.co.uk/jcurry/) was far more informative and not restricted to sanitised information. Web anarchy rules!

LEISUREPLAN   http://www.leisureplan.com

View colour photos of over 13,000 hotels before you make a reservation. Links allow you to search for the lowest plane fares, rent a car, book transport at your destination, plan a cruise, get hints and detailed destination descriptions, plan a trip, then book everything on-line – easy!

MAPQUEST   http://www.mapquest.com/

Almost every major city in the world – and a few of the smaller ones – are in MapQuest's database. The level of detail ranges from large-scale plans showing major routes in and out to individual streets, with locations of important facilities (hotels, theatres, banks etc) shown. There are also links to other resources – weather, restaurants, accommodation, local information and so forth. The maps can be printed and come out best on a decent colour printer.

MULTI MEDIA MAPPING   http://uk.multimap.com/howto.htm

This is a wonderful idea – UK maps within your web pages. Provide surfers with a map showing the places described on your pages or include a small map in your page, showing the places the page relates to, such as your address or general area. The only information needed is the full postcode embedded in a link. This is a free service, but larger maps, individual support etc are available for a fee.

RAC   http://www.rac.co.uk/

Anyone planning a road trip should access route planning and then traffic news. The print-out of route, distance, times and traffic alerts will speed your journey no end. The main part of the site – called Digital Services – is an excellent example of complicated information handled simply and well.

ROUGH GUIDE   http://www.roughguides.com

Like Fodor's and Berlitz, Rough Guides are well known in their print format. The web guide is amazing. There are more than 3,500 places on the database and an excellent search engine to reach them. A related e-zine site has more in-depth articles on many of these and there are excellent tips for the traveller and visitor. An e-mail newsletter (free) will keep you updated. Good visuals make the site a joy to use.

TERRASERVER   http://www.terraserver.com/

Oh yes! Images from Russian spy satellites. Type in your location or click on a map and home in on your home. Or anyone else's. Good images of natural resources (Niagara Falls, volcanos), well-known buildings and whole cities. This is better than any map.

TOURISM OFFICES WORLDWIDE   http://www.towd.com

This is another one of those obvious but great ideas: a listing of tourist offices by destination and – extremely useful – where to find one country's offices in another country. There are also links to country and destination web sites and other contact information (phone, fax etc). In combination with the Rough Guide (above) it makes planning a trip a pleasure instead of a logistical nightmare. What makes the web site itself attractive is the lack of advertising and annoying banners and pop-ups.

TRAVEL RESOURCES   http://www.travel-resources.com

Not every guidebook can tell you everything. Sometimes the best tips come from others who have travelled before. And that's what this site is – a grab-bag of useful and relevant information about a country, city or region with links others have discovered that will be useful. Pay back the compliment – leave your own favourite links on the site and keep it growing.

VIRTUAL LONDON — http://www.a-london-guide.co.uk

The site is aimed at visitors to London rather than natives, but even for the latter there is useful information. Theatre schedules, events listings (with contact details), places to stay with a reservation facility and various other helpful features (like the Cockney–English dictionary) make it possible to plan an entire trip. The links section is comprehensive and contains all the attractions you would expect plus a few surprising ones. The web cam check-the-weather facility is puzzling – why is it in Acton rather than, say, Marble Arch and does the lady opposite know it can see right into her living room? Still, it claims to be the first web cam in the UK, although the Cambridge Coffee Pot people (http://web.wt.net/~bparker/coffee.htm) might dispute that.

There are simply too many electronic magazines (e-zines) in too many categories and catering for too diverse a range of specialist interests to make any sensible choice as to quality. Below is a list of sites where on-line magazines can be found to cater for any interest or taste.

ELECTRONIC NEWSTAND   http://www.enews.com/

This is a comprehensive, searchable collection of over 2,000 on-line magazines. It includes Off The Rack, an e-zine about e-zines, and a customisation feature so you can be informed about updates in your area of interest.

E-ZINE LIST   http://www.meer.net/~johnl/e-zine-list/

This list of e-zines from all around the world, accessible via the web, FTP, e-mail and other methods, is updated approximately monthly.

MAGAZINE ISSUES   http://www.freeandfun.com/freestuff/magazines.html

This is not e-zines as such, but an electronic list of conventional magazines which give out free trial issues, posted to your home address.

ZINES   http://www.ezconnect.com/magk.htm

EZ Connect's list of e-zines is thorough and easy to search.

GUIDE TO ONLINE WEB MAGAZINES   http://www.webreference.com/

Webreference maintains a list of e-zines related to the web and generally for web authors, designers and programmers. However, other e-zine lists are available within. It is expecially good on e-commerce and internet marketing.

NEWBIES GUIDE TO E-ZINES   http://www.mbn-businesscomplex.net/newbieguide.html

Fancy setting up your own electronic publication? This page contains a free, downloadable guide to setting up an e-zine. It contains much invaluable information and some which should be taken with a pinch of salt. But overall, it's worth the 1Mb download and a read.

Does this merit a section of its own? If the number of hits *Star Trek* sites accumulate is anything to go by, this is one of the most popular subjects on the web. There are now more speakers of Klingon than of Esperanto. The sites vary in nature and content, some are 'official' (i.e. owned or sanctioned by the producers or licensed merchandisers) and some maintained by afficionados, often using images of questionable legality in terms of copyright. I am grateful to Jason Filer in South Africa, for his excellent guidance to the best and brightest, boldly going beyond frontiers no one has gone beyond before. Those below are chosen for their excellence of informational content, design, functionality and appeal to Trekkies, Trekkers and others.

General sites

JAMJARS STAR TREK SITE   http://mzone.mweb.co.za/residents/jfiler/stlinks.html

Absolutely everything is somewhere on this encyclopaedic web site.

STAR TREK CONTINUUM   http://www.startrek.com

The official site (see page 122).

BRAVO FLEET   http://www.bravofleet.com

The best e-mail sim on the web.

WARP CORE AWARDS   http://mainengineering.simplenet.com/warp_core_award.html

So what are the best *Trek* sites? See for yourself.

NEXUS   http://members.aol.com/treknexus/trektopk.htm

The ultimate guide to all things *Star Trek* on the net.

STAR TREK – THE COMIC STRIP   http://www.sev.com.au/toonzone/sevtrek.htm

John Cook's iconoclastic take-off cartoon strip.

STAR TREK NEWSLETTER http://members.aol.com/jos42/stgn

Galactic e-mail!

STEVE'S TREK PAGE http://soli.inav.net/~nibblink/trek.htm

Personal access and a personal view of the series.

LINDA'S VOYAGER PAGE http://www.geocities.com/hollywood/trailer/3687/startrek.html

One for the Janeway fans.

THE STAR TREK ARCHIVE http://www.cs.umanitoba.ca/~djc/startrek/

For anyone into the technical side, this is a great canon site.

SOUNDSTONE http://www.soundstone.com/scripts/index.cfm?rfd=3413&rfn=1

Purchasing the soundtracks of *Trek*.

Web rings

FEDERATIONS WEBRING http://www.geocities.com/Area51/Hollow/2909/

Jason Filer from South Africa is something of a Trek fan. This is his own web ring, with an e-mail role-playing group.

ENTERPRISE – E WEB RING http://www.geocities.com/area51/cavern/2135/

Another of Jason Filer's rings, this one has 4,000 members, and is growing fast.

STAR TREK VOYAGER RING http://www.geocities.com/petsburgh/5777/vring.html

Just what it says.

LOCUTUS' ASSIMILATION RING http://lcars.simplenet.com/ring/

This claims to be the largest *Trek* ring on the web. Resistance is futile, apparently.

UNITED FEDERATION OF PAGES http://members.aol.com/ufppres1/index.htm

Another of the same.

Other sites

RECENT EPISODES   http://kcohn.simplenet.com/alidarjarok/

Alidar Jarok's Star Trek Recent Episodes Image Library is well put together.

STARFLEET DATABASE: CHRONOLOGY   http://www.geocities.com/area51/cavern/6053

An interesting site for continuity freaks.

UTOPIA PLANETIA   http://stzone.simplenet.com/utopia/

An interesting 'non-canon' tech site.

TREK ART   http://www.netcomuk.co.uk/~trekart

Full colour schematics.

NEMRAC   http://members.aol.com/nemrac47/bigship.htm

An Excelsior cut-away schematic.

DEEP SPACE 14   http://www.ping.be/ds14/

Another site for ship schematics and other technical info.

Technical sites

There are dozens, if not hundreds, but among the best for data and specs on the vessels of *Star Trek* and *Star Wars* are:

LCARS:FEDERATION DATABANK   http://welcome.to/lcars
DAYSTROM INSTITUTE TECHNICAL LIBRARY
    http://www.adeadend.demon.co.uk
THE STARSHIP ENCYCLOPEDIA
    http://www.pacificnet.net/~filmman/starships/picard.html
LCARS STAR TREK DATABASE V4.0   http://privat.schlund.de/ncc2051/
UTOPIA PLANITIA STARSHIP DATABASE
    http://www.behaviour.co.uk/utopia/planitia/
202129 RESOURCE CENTER
    http://www.geocities.com/area51/dimension/4733

Visual resources

ON SCREEN	http://www.eclipse.co.uk/onscreen
DIGITAL STREAM	http://www.digistream.com/g_startrek.htm

New special effects for *Star Trek: TOS*.

PEDRO'S SHIPORAMA	http://www.shiporama.org
SPACE:THE FINAL FRONTIER	http://www.geocities.com/hollywood/hills/1960
THE STAR TREK COLLECTIVE	http://goldenmillion.com/thegalaxy

Video clips, sounds, spoilers and images.

ST-INSURRECTION.COM	http://www.st-insurrection.com

Get a glimpse of the latest movie.

WARP CORE	http://z-core.simplenet.com/warpcore/

One of the largest *Star Trek* picture archives.

STAR TREK THE ORIGINAL SERIES	http://www.safelink.net/danrose/startrek.html

A photo gallery of Kirk and friends.

Aliens

ALIEN ARCHIVES	http://www.geocities.com/hollywood/academy/7086/

Take a look here for everything alien.

QUARK'S PLACE	http://www.orlinter.com/users/grandnag/default.htm

Take a break at Quark's but make sure you know the Farengi
Rules of Aquisition (available to the earthbound at
http://www.greatbasin.net/~knockahomer/trekpage.html).

GUINAN'S BAR AND GRILLE http://www.geocities.com/area51/chamber/2541

Stop by if you are in need of refreshment.

ROMULAN STAR EMPIRE http://www.homeworld.com

For all fans of Romulans, this is the place to go.

IMPERIAL DATABASE http://home.att.net/~masrotaj/

The site of the Klingon Defence Forces.

KLINGON IMPERIAL DIPLOMATIC CORPS http://www.klingon.org

The representatives of the empire here on Earth.

KHITOMER COMMAND CENTER http://www.geocities.com/area51/dunes/2245

Good Klingon site.

IMPERIAL WEAPONS GUIDE http://www.geocities.com/area51/nebula/5094/

Data on Klingon weapons.

BAJORAN RESOURCE CENTRE http://www.webcon.net.au/bajor/

A wealth of info on all things Bajoran.

Klingon language

KLINGON RESOURCES
  http://labs.thomtech.com/~dspeers/klingon/resources.htm
KLINGON LANGUAGE INSTITUTE http://www.kli.org
KLINGON LANGUAGE CLAN http://usskatana.ml.org/~klc/

One of the commonest criticisms levelled at the web is its high proportion of complete nonsense. However, some of it is genuinely fascinating, if pointless, and no one is forced to browse it. And what harm does it do? Divert yourself with the folly of misplaced human endeavour and then ponder whether most is more or less worthwhile than many other things that are presented to you daily, some of them dressed up as high art, situation comedy, computer manuals or editorials in supposedly serious newspapers.

APRIL FOOL   http://www.aprilfool.com

To say too much about this site would give it away. Suffice to say there are great surprises and practical jokes for children of all ages, especially the ones who haunt office parties with a whoopee cushion.

FISHYDANCE   http://www.fishydance.com/index.htm

This is a site with no point whatsoever. Pictures of fish dancing to a tune of your choice. Pick 'Fish Heads' for the best of these. Then go quietly mad.

DILBERT   http://www.dilbert.com/

Apart from the cartoons, there are amusing sidelines such as having your mission statement written by Catbert, daily mental workouts and other forms of corporate anarchy. The original 50 Dilbert strips from Scott Adams are here, too. Links to other comic strips are comprehensive – good to see The Wizard of Id still going, for example.

ROLLERCOASTER   http://www.echonyc.com/~dne/rollercoaster!/

This is deeply strange – a site dedicated to classic rollercoasters, ancient and modern, and an apologia entitled 'Why We Ride'. The Least Terrifying Ride Ever is 'The Sky Princess' and you are surely a better person for knowing that.

GIBBLETOONS   http://www.gibbleguts.com/daily.htm

If Gary Larson is possessed and Dilbert an anarchist, then Dan Gibson is fit for tying up. The Daily Gibblefix is now on my browser's opening page but humour is an individual thing. Not one for the children or servants.

HEROIC STORIES   http://www.heroicstories.com/

Randy Cassingham has published This is True, one of the largest free subscription newsletters on the internet, weekly since 1994. It reports bizarre-but-true stories and headlines from the world's press. This new venture intends to publicise good things that people do, which may not make it into the newspapers, such as How Mr Sulu Talked Me Out Of Smoking. One to watch, definitely.

GLASBERGEN   http://www.glasbergen.com/

Randy Glasbergen probably isn't in the Scott Adams and Garfield stakes as a renowned cartoonist, but his site is a sterling effort at turning an honest buck out of merchandising his cartoons. They are genuinely funny and deserve a visit. The education cartoons are a good resource for teachers wishing to make a point or two in a lesson or study guide.

NIMBY   http://www.notinmybackyard.com/

Nicely designed as a framed cartoon with clickable links, this site has some intruging features – the Artist link leads to one of the strangest but most effective rollover graphics on the web. The Doghouse has clipart and colouring activities for children.

NATIONAL COUNCIL FOR DULL MEN   http://www.dullmen.com/links.htm

This admirable and worthy body has collected the web's most boring sites and presents them here for your edification. The site contains some true classics – the Empire State Building Webcam, Marmite on Everything and How to Rake Leaves are good examples – but the Cambridge Coffee Pot (see page 170) has a cult status all of its own. Link to the Boring Institute (http://www.boringinstitute.com/) and discover the most boring celebrities.

THE NATIONAL ANXIETY CENTER http://www.anxietycenter.com/

'The Good News is that the Bad News is wrong!' The Earth is fine, there is no global warming, America has 28 per cent more standing timber than in 1952, the world has infinite capacity to deal with garbage and crime rates continue to decline. Now, isn't that nice?

UEXPRESS http://www.uexpress.com/ups/

This predictable site from United Press Syndicate has little to recommend it, except the Cheap Psychological Tricks feature, which are mostly short quizzes with baffling analyses by a psychologist that reveal nothing valuable whatsoever.

ROYAL INSIGHT http://www.royalinsight.gov.uk/

How is it, that when Her Maj can get it so right in her own site (see The British Monarchy, http://www.royal.gov.uk/, page 42), this official site can get it so depressingly wrong? This is *Hello* meets *Down Your Way* and reduces some rather important and dignified activities to the status of a freakshow. But taken in that vein, it's good for a laugh. Ask a question, like 'Can Her Majesty cook?' and get an ostensibly straight answer.

Somebody may be watching you on the web right now. There are many, many internet cameras out there. This section lists 20 or so of the best views.

UK

CAIRNGORM http://www.phy.hw.ac.uk/resrev/aws/weather.htm

Breathtaking vistas from the summit of one of Scotland's highest mountains, courtesy of Heriot-Watt University, Edinburgh.

EDINBURGH http://www.scotsman.com/

Views of the world's most beautiful city from the roof of *The Scotsman* newspaper building.

LONDON http://news.bbc.co.uk/hi/english/static/domecam/default.htm

The BBC's camera at Britain's Millennium Dome in Greenwick, London.

LOCH NESS MONSTER CAM http://www.lochness.co.uk

If there is anything more pointless than gazing at the UK's largest stretch of water for sight of an aquatic myth, it is gazing at a monitor to see a web cam gazing at the UK's largest stretch of water etc etc. Still, there are streaming video 'live eyewitness reports' and a good gallery of the 'best' pictures of Nessie, whether you believe them or not.

International

SAN FRANCISCO http://citynight.com/camera

City Of Night, the first live and publicly telerobotic internet camera in San Francisco (actually in Alameda) has operated since 1995 and offers stunning views of the Bay Area, which you can direct.

ANTARTICA http://www.antdiv.gov.au/stations/live.html

This Australian Government camera shows live views from four research stations at Casey, Davis, Mawson and Macquarie Island.

BUENOS AIRES, ARGENTINA http://www.lanacion.com.ar/espec/camaras/98/index2.htm

Zoom, move and direct the interactive view of this beautiful city.

MELBOURNE, AUSTRALIA

http://melbourne.citysearch.com.au/melbourne/weather/melbourne_web_cam/

There are 32 different views in the Melbourne area from here.

VANCOUVER, CANADA http://www.telemark.net/cgi-shl/wc.pl

Katcam gives one of the most stunning views in the world.

PARIS, FRANCE http://www.tf1.fr/cgi-bin/tf1/maj.cgi?livecam&sommairefr.htm

View the Seine river and the Eiffel Tower, then move the camera and see more of the City of Lights, courtesy of Television France 1.

SINGAPORE http://www.mediacity.com.sg/skycam/

At last a benevolent use for traffic cameras. The live streams require NetShow to view but the different scenes around Singapore are worth it.

SWITZERLAND http://naturaplan.coop.ch/d/oeko/kamunit.htm

This site has links to various web cams at Swiss farms including one with real-time 360 degree pan and zoom control.

BELGRADE, YUGOSLAVIA http://www.inet.co.yu/kamera/

Live streaming views of central Belgrade.

WUPPERTAL , GERMANY   http://www.wuppertal-forum.de/wupper/live.htm

The Schwebebahn Railway in Wuppertal is famous, like Londons buses or San Francisco's cablecars.

BUDAPEST, HUNGARY   http://www.internetto.hu/kamera/fullsize.html

Views of the worlds second most beautiful city, looking towards the Citadel.

HONG KONG   http://netvigator.com/~dbhk/html/office.html

Eight to 10 cameras (it varies) including a 3-D version.

FLORENCE, ITALY   http://www.vps.it/florence/

Apart from the live cam, there is good information on Florentine history back to Roman times.

MT FUJI, JAPAN   http://www.city.fujiyoshida.yamanashi.jp/mtfuji/tonbo/index-e.html

This real-time interactive camera is controllable to give great views of the famous mountain scenery.

MT EVEREST, NEPAL   http://www.m.chiba-u.ac.jp/class/respir/ismm98.htm

Because it's there.

PANAMA CANAL   http://www.pancanal.com/photo/camera-java.html

This camera shows the locks of the canal from a high tower.

ST. PETERSBURG, RUSSIA   http://www.metrocam.ru/Company/Misc/camera-eng.htm

A view of the Nevsky Prospekt, the principal street of Russia's ancient capital.

Just weird

REAL FRIDGE CAM   http://www.electrolux.com/show.asp?id=168

This is just weird. To quote: 'For the first time in history, a live camera will reveal the secret life of groceries and other consumer products that dwell in a fridge. See red relaxed tomatoes relaxing in the grocery box. Study the social life of lemon yogurts and speculate on the thoughts of assorted groceries. Await with excitement the next grand opening... who will open the door? Mummy? Daddy, one of the sisters? The cat?' If this is intentional it is very funny and excellently conceived. If it's serious, somebody needs a long holiday.

There is a great deal of nonsense out there that goes beyond the surreal category. Some of it is intentional nonsense, some of it means well and some people ought to know better. Corporate and business web sites are excluded from this evaluation because nobody likes a law suit. Enjoy.

BODY MAGIC   http://www.eventmediagroup.com/bodymagic/

Contortionists abound in this site dedicated to the noble art of getting your leg round behind your ears. Stunning pictures.

THE BUREAU OF MISSING SOCKS   http://www.jagat.com/joel/socks.html

I do not believe the web site will exist by the time you read this, but nevertheless... The 'official' department on the web for information regarding lost socks has an area dedicated to single socks longing to meet others. A worthy cause.

THE CORPORATION   http://www.thecorporation.com/home.html

Who is The Corporation? A bunch of anarchists determined to make the web fun, that's who. Apparently, we are all employees. Better check to see what your bosses are up to. The site includes a gallery of 'interesting' corporate slogans. Designed like a real corporate site any multinational would be proud of, it's hard to tell the difference.

FLYPOWER   http://www.flypower.com

This site is all about paper aeroplanes powered by house flies. There are regular Tech Updates on new research and development projects and an 'Alternate Engines Page'. Bzzz. Excellent design and graphics by people of real, if misguided, talent.

KISSTHISGUY.COM   http://www.kissthisguy.com/index.html

Ever misheard a song then sang it on a bus? Embarrassing. This site is dedicated to all of us who thought Sting was singing 'I'm a lethal idiot'. There is a huge collection of wrong songs (and the right versions) including the famouus Hendrix misquote used in the site title. Clever use of frames and databases make this site a joy to browse.

MARS WEST   http://www.marswest.org

Of course you can go to Mars, dear. Be back for tea-time, though. These people are ready and they want you to come too!

THE MUSEUM OF DIRT   http://www.planet.com/dirtweb/dirt.html

Strangely, this site didn't make it into the museums section (page 139) but where else could you examine dirt samples from far away places, including Eurodisney and celebrities' gardens?

READING BAR CODES   http://www.pixi.com/~owens/barcodes/index.html

---

I have always wanted to be able to read barcodes and now, I am none the wiser.

THE RUBBER CHICKEN   http://www.rubberchicken.com/

This is the place for practical jokes and other gags. There are also numerous links to other like-minded sites.

THE SECRET DIARY OF BILL GATES   http://www.billg.org/secretdiary/main/index.htm

---

Well, I'd sue. This is so realistic it is hard not to take seriously. What do you want to read today? It includes an appeal by the site designer for more work that is so outrageous that every other webbie should adopt it.

TEMP 24-7   http://www.temp247.com/live/issue/current/home_frames.html

---

This is a site for temps, straight from the heart. Play the Shockwave game Temps v Suits – hurl office equipment at well-known bosses then attack the boardroom and fight a tribe of rabid Chief Execs. More fun than Doom. Then contribute to Temp Tales of Terror (share the pain).

WILLS ON THE WEB http://www.ca-probate.com/wills.htm

Want to see the will of Jackie Kennedy? How about Jerry Garcia (of sound mind, it seems), Elvis Presley or the Princess of Wales? The famous, infamous and not famous at all are here, if anyone's interested.

WWWASTE OF TIME http://www.accessv.com/~georged/wwwasteoftime

'Dedicated to the noble pursuit of wasting everybody's time on-line' – the site lives up to its name. A neat feature is a 'Here Comes The Boss!' hyperlink to a real commercial web site. Or not. It's your risk. Who said the Canadians had no sense of humour?

COUNTRY COWGIRL http://www.geocities.com/heartland/plains/5811/

For sheer self-indulgence, this site can't be beat. If you are into jam-making, golden labradors, community action, motherhood and apple pie, visit here and see what it looks like from the perspective of downhome America.

SUPERBAD http://www.superbad.com/

I have *no idea* what this site is about. If you want to see what people apparently waste their time doing with web sites, this is as good a place to start as any. Sub-sites are dedicated to bathroom wallpaper, Ford Pintos and sundry other whimsy.

GVOON http://www.gvoon.de

Don't ask! Just do it!

Every writer needs help – some more than others. This section features useful on-line style and grammar guides, dictionaries and thesauri, plus on-line tools for writers in addition to those listed in Reference (page 64), plus some links to useful writers' pages.

RESOURCES FOR WRITERS   http://www.cohums.ohio-state.edu/english/facstf/kol/write.htm

---

This site has many links to other useful on-line tools for writers and is a very good starting point for a lot of other material.

WRITER'S RESOURCES ON THE WEB http://www.interlog.com/~ohi/www/writesource.html

---

This is another facet of the WWW Virtual Library. Their Guide to Writing Resources on the Web has a large section on writing as a craft and includes grammar and style guides.

BUSINESS AND PROFESSIONAL COMMUNICATION

http://www.cohums.ohio-state.edu/english/areas/bizcom.htm

Business English is a language in itself, with its own rules and expectations. For those interested in business communications and writing for businesses, this site has links to web sites which deal with such issues.

COMMON GRAMMAR, USAGE, & SPELLING PROBLEMS

http://theodore-sturgeon.mit.edu:8001/uu-gna/text/wamt/acchtml/gram1.html

---

Trust MIT to name a web server after one of the greatest SciFi authors. Appropriately, this page has an on-line guide to common grammar and spelling problems – colons, apostrophes, capitals – necessarily from an American perspective, but useful nevertheless.

JACK LYNCH'S GRAMMAR AND STYLE NOTES

http://www.english.upenn.edu/~jlynch/grammar.html

Jack Lynch is the University of Pennsylvania writing guru. He has collected his class notes on grammatical rules, style and

usage into a web site. Somewhat miscellaneous, it is
nonetheless a good read for those who would like to
understand the *why* of grammar.

ROGET'S THESAURUS SEARCH FORM

http://humanities.uchicago.edu/forms_unrest/roget.html

This form-based interface to the best-known thesaurus can be
searched by 'headwords' or text.

HYPERTEXT WEBSTER INTERFACE
http://c.gp.cs.cmu.edu:5103/prog/webster?

This is another form-based dictionary interface, this time to
Websters' (American), but it is extremely complete.

This listing is taken from Web21 (http://web21.com). Web21 ranks sites by page views ('traffic') but groups web sites into families (such as all the Warner Brothers sites). They ignore adult sites, ISPs and colleges. However, a lot of the most-visited sites are, as you might expect, search engines and directories.

This listing was correct for the day it was taken, but the Web21 page will have the latest. However, certain things stand out:

AOL and Netscape are equal first. At the time of writing these were due to merge. Each gets more hits than Microsoft.

Yahoo! appears to be the most-used search engine, along with the Four11 people finder. Most of the other search engines are about the same in terms of hits.

Download.com appears to be the biggest freeware, shareware and commercial software site in terms of visits.

The way to get people to your site is to offer something really useful, really free – Netscape and WinZip are excellent examples of this.

Each of these sites is worth a visit – an immense number of hits must mean something.

Rank	Site	URL1
1	AOL.COM and	http://www.aol.com
	NETSCAPE	http://home.netscape.com
2	YAHOO!	http://www.yahoo.com
	and FOUR11	http://www.four11.com
3	MICROSOFT CORP.	http://www.microsoft.com
	including MSN.COM and	http://www.msn.com
	LINKEXCHANGE	http://www.linkexchange.com
4	GO.COM WORLD NETWORK	http://www.go.com
5	ALTAVISTA SEARCH ENGINE,	http://www.altavista.digital.com
	COMPAQ, and TANDEM	http://www.compaq.com
		http://www.tandem.com
6	LYCOS SEARCH ENGINE,	http://www.lycos.com
	POINT, and WHO WHERE	http://www.pointcom.com
		http://www.whowhere.com
7	EXCITE, MAGELLAN, CITY.NET,	http://www.excite.com
	and WEBCRAWLER	http://www.mckinley.com
		http://www.city.net

		http://www.webcrawler.com
8	XOOM	http://www.xoom.com
9	CNN INTERACTIVE	http://www.cnn.com
10	BESEEN.COM – HELPING BUILD WEB COMMUNITIES WORLDWIDE!	http://www.beseen.com
11	CNET, SEARCH.COM, NEWS.COM, and DOWNLOAD.COM	http://www.cnet.com http://www.search.com http://www.news.com http://www.download.com
12	BLUE MOUNTAIN ARTS' ELECTRONIC GREETING CARDS	http://www.bluemountain.com
13	THE GO2NET NETWORK and 100HOT	http://www.go2net.com http://www.100hot.com
14	MACROMEDIA	http://www.macromedia.com
15	SONY, SONY MUSIC, THE STATION, SONY COMPUTER ENTERTAINMENT	http://www.sony.com http://www.music.sony.com http://www.station.sony.com http://www.scea.sony.com
16	PATHFINDER and WARNER BROS. SITES	http://www.pathfinder.com http://www.warnerbros.com
17	IMAGINE MEDIA	http://www.imaginemedia.com
18	FREE SITES NETWORK	http://www.fsn.net
19	INFOSPACE.COM	http://www.infospace.com
20	CBS SPORTSLINE	http://www.sportsline.com
21	SPORTING LIFE ONLINE	http://www.sporting-life.com
22	NETADDRESS	http://netaddress.usa.net
23	REALNETWORKS (REALAUDIO and REALVIDEO)	http://www.real.com
24	INTERNET MOVIE DATABASE and the UK EDITION	http://www.imdb.com http://uk.imdb.com
25	FILEZ: FREEWARE, SHAREWARE and SOFTWARE	http://www.filez.com
26	AUDIOFIND – MULTIMEDIA SEARCH ENGINE	http://www.audiofind.com
27	TUCOWS and FREETHEMES	http://www.tucows.com http://www.freethemes.com
28	NETTAXI COMMUNITY	http://www.nettaxi.com
29	BOMIS	http://www.bomis.com
30	PHONELINK.PLC	http://www.phonelink.com
31	DOGPILE (MULTI-ENGINE SEARCH TOOL)	http://www.dogpile.com
32	DEJANEWS	http://www.dejanews.com

33	ZIFF DAVIS, HOTFILES	http://www.zdnet.com
	and ZDU.COM	http://www.hotfiles.com
		http://www.zdu.com
34	INFOBEAT	http://www.infobeat.com
35	THE CREATIVE ZONE!	http://www.creaf.com
36	USA TODAY	http://www.usatoday.com
37	ATTITUDE NETWORK: HAPPY	http://www.attitude.net
	PUPPY and GAMES DOMAIN	http://www.happypuppy.com
		http://www.gamesdomain.com
38	LOOKSMART	http://www.looksmart.com
39	THE GLOBE ONLINE COMMUNITY	http://www.theglobe.com
40	UPROAR! FREE GAMES – WIN PRIZES!	http://www.uproar.com
41	ASK JEEVES HOME	http://www.askjeeves.com
42	FINDMAIL EGROUPS.COM	http://www.egroups.com
43	EBAY AUCTION CLASSIFIEDS	http://www.ebay.com
44	CARD4YOU.COM	http://www.card4you.com
45	GALORE SEARCH ENGINE	http://www.galore.com
46	NEWSNOW	http://www.newsnow.co.uk
47	GRAND CENTRAL STATION @ FORTUNECITY	http://www.fortunecity.com
48	SKYTEL	http://www.skytel.com
49	GOTO.COM (SEARCHING)	http://www.goto.com
50	BEFIRST.NET	http://www.befirst.net
51	IBM CORPORATION	http://www.ibm.com
52	WINFILES.COM and	http://www.winfiles.com
	VSERVERS.COM	http://www.vservers.com
53	MP3.COM	http://www.mp3.com
54	ECHELON ENTERTAINMENT	http://www.eesite.com
55	SUN MICROSYSTEMS and	http://www.sun.com
	SUN'S JAVA SITE	http://java.sun.com
56	GAMESPOT	http://www.gamespot.com
57	BLOOMBERG ONLINE	http://www.bloomberg.com
58	MECKLERMEDIA'S INTERNET.COM	http://www.internet.com
59	TOM'S HARDWARE	http://www.tomshardware.com
60	WINZIP	http://www.winzip.com
61	INTEL CORP.	http://www.intel.com
62	APPLE COMPUTER, INC.	http://www.apple.com
63	THE REALNAME SYSTEM	http://www.realnames.com
	BY CENTRAAL CORPORATION	
64	MONSTER.COM	http://www.monster.com
65	UGO, including: GAMEPEN,	http://www.ugo.net

	GAME REVOLUTION, and	http://www.gamepen.com
	GAME DEPOT	http://www.game-revolution.com
		http://www.gamedemo.com
66	CARLINGNET	http://www.carlingnet.com
67	SLASHDOT	http://www.slashdot.org/
68	THE NEW YORK TIMES	http://www.nytimes.com
69	PERSONALS – ONE & ONLY – HOME PAGE	http://www.one-and-only.com
70	CARDMASTER	http://www.cardmaster.com
71	WESTWOOD STUDIOS	http://www.westwood.com
72	MTV ONLINE	http://www.mtv.com
73	MP3 DIRECT DOWNLOAD ARCHIVE	http://www.mp3dda.com
74	TIMES MIRROR INTERZINES	http://www.tminterzines.com
75	BLIZZARD ENTERTAINMENT NEWS	http://www.blizzard.com
76	NEXTCARD	http://www.nextcard.com
77	ANDY'S ART ATTACK!	http://www.andyart.com
78	SPACEPORTS.COM	http://www.spaceports.com
79	IDG.NET	http://www.idg.net
80	WINAMP	http://www.winamp.com
81	SANDER'S SCREEN SAVERS PREVIEWER	http://www.screensavershot.com
82	CHANNEL 1 CHATHOUSE and	http://www.chathouse.com
	FILELIBRARY	http://www.filelibrary.com
83	3COM	http://www.3com.com
84	FXWEB	http://www.fxweb.com
85	TY.COM	http://www.ty.com
86	AS	http://www.as.org/
87	DISCOVERY ONLINE	http://www.discovery.com
88	AT HAND QUICK SEARCH	http://www.athand.com
89	123GREETINGS	http://www.123greetings.com
90	ANIME WEB TURNPIKE	http://www.anipike.com
91	AMAZON.COM	http://www.amazon.com
92	BOLT	http://www.bolt.com
93	GAMESCENE	http://www.gamescene.com
94	PANASONIC	http://www.panasonic.com
95	CMPNET	http://www.cmpnet.com
96	ONELIST	http://www.onelist.com
97	FREE-GRAPHICS.COM	http://www.free-graphics.com
98	DAVECENTRAL (SHAREWARE, FREEWARE, DEMOS)	http://www.davecentral.com
99	DRUDGE REPORT®	http://www.drudgereport.com
100	NOKIA ON THE WEB	http://www.nokia.com

ActiveX Microsoft's own programming components inserted into a web page to provide functions not available in HTML, such as video clips, on-line ordering and payments, or database access. ActiveX comes from two other Microsoft technologies called Component Object Modelling (COM) and Object Linking and Embedding (OLE). It applies to a whole set of COM-based technologies but is loosely used for ActiveX controls, a specific implementation of ActiveX. ActiveX controls can be implemented in a number of programming languages. This (like Java) allows considerable interactivity within web pages. It is specific to Internet Explorer (Windows 95/NT and later), but the Ncompass plug-in allows embedded ActiveX controls to work in Netscape.

Adobe Acrobat Programs developed by Adobe Systems for creating and distributing documents electronically as Portable Document Format (PDF) files. These can be viewed with the Acrobat Reader. The Acrobat Reader, the best known Acrobat component, is freely available as a stand-alone program or a *plug-in*.

Applet A small application (program) run from within another program, not directly from the operating system. The best known examples are *Java* applets.

Avatar A graphic which represents a real person in a cyberspace system and which the user can direct to change depending on what they are doing (talking, walking, etc.). It is also another name, like root, for the superuser account on UNIX systems.

Banner Originally, an advertisement displayed on the results page of a *search engine*, generated in response to the searched term. Advertisers pay to have their ads displayed when keywords are searched by a browser ('keyword advertising'). Banners can also be inserted into web pages, using a Banner Ad Manager, which handles transitions of one ad to the next, usually timed. See also *banner exchange*.

Banner exchange Web site designers or owners can agree to exchange *banner* ads with each other, thereby increasing the likelihood their product or service will be seen by browsers. There are many Banner Exchange Programmes which will arrange this.

Bookmark Confusingly, there are two usages: One is a placeholder in a document – anyone familiar with word processing will have used these. The second is a feature which allows a web *browser* to save the address (*URL*) of a web page as a shortcut so it can be re-visited. These are called Bookmarks in Netscape and *Favorites* in Internet Explorer. See Appendix for more detail.

Browser A web browser is an application which interprets the commands which make up a web page and displays the page as designed. The two most popular are Netscape Navigator and Microsoft Internet Explorer. These are graphical browsers, which display images as well as text.

Most modern browsers can present *multimedia*, though they may require *plug-ins*.

Browsing Finding and viewing web pages with a web *browser*. Searching the web for specific subjects.

Bulletin board An electronic message centre, usually for specific interests. Users *dial up*, read messages left by others and leave their replies or new messages. Bulletin board systems (BBSs) are a good place to find cheap or free software. There are many tens of thousands of BBSs worldwide.

Button In graphical user interfaces like Windows, a small outlined area or graphic in a box that selects a command or option when clicked. Do not confuse with a mouse button.

CAD Computer-aided design – a general name for programs which allow the manipulation of two-dimensional and three-dimensional graphics as an aid to design.

cgi See *common gateway interface*.

cgi script See *common gateway interface*.

Clipart Electronic illustrations provided in collections for insertion into a document or web page. Most clipart packages provide illustrations in several file formats (bmp, *gif, jpeg,* wmf) so they can be used in various word-processing applications.

Common gateway interface A specification for transferring information between a web *server* and a cgi program designed to accept and return data, such as form processing. The browser sends data to a cgi 'script' (program) on the *server*, the script integrates the data with a database held on the server and the results are sent back as HTML to a web page. These cgi scripts can be written in many programming languages such as C++, Perl, Java or Visual Basic, and many examples are freely available (see page 90). Other methods of achieving this are ISAPI (Internet Server Application Programming Interface, used by Microsoft) and NSAPI (Netscape Server Application Programming Interface).

Cookie A message sent to a *browser* by a web server. The browser stores the message in a file usually called cookie.txt and the message is sent back to the server each time the browser requests a page from that server. This allows the server to identify users and send them customised web pages, such as a welcome message with your name in it. The name stems from UNIX programming objects called 'magic cookies', tokens attached to a user or program which change according to the areas entered. There are ways to disable cookies or prevent them sending any meaningful information (see page 100).

Dial-up The mechanism which connects your computer via a modem to a Point of Presence (POP) and logs into your *internet service provider (ISP)*. The ISP provides information, such as the gateway address, and may need your computer's IP address. See also *domain name*.

Directory A folder which holds a series of related files on a computer. See also *directory list*.

Directory list A style of HTML formatting for web pages, usually presented as a bulleted list of items. Different browsers present these in different ways and some ignore the style completely.

Domain name A name, such as mysite.co.uk, which identifies one or more IP addresses and takes the place of the actual IP address (such as 215.22.132.34). Every domain name has a suffix that indicates which top-level domain (.com, .net, .ac, etc.) it belongs to. There are only a limited number of such domains. Domain names can be bought and registered.

Dongle There are two definitions. One refers to a small hardware device attached to a computer which controls access to a particular application, as a form of software licence protection. The dongle is usually attached to the PC's parallel printer port. However, it has also come to mean any software that provides a small but useful piece of functionality, such as a *cgi* script.

Download Copying data from a main source to a peripheral device, such as copying a file from an on-line service or a network file *server* to a local computer. It is also used to mean the process of loading a font into a laser printer's memory. The opposite of download is upload, which means to copy a file from your own computer to another computer.

Drag and drop Applications which allow the user to drag objects, using the mouse, to other locations on the screen, such as pulling a *link* from a web page to the PC's desktop. Modern operating systems like Windows allow drag and drop between applications. The user can create a picture with a graphics package and drag it into a word processor document or web page.

Dynamic HTML A way of making the web page change according to the user's interaction. It goes beyond standard HTML to provide functions which make web pages richer and more interesting. See page 3.

E-business This is the overall term for conducting business *on-line*. It includes, but goes beyond, *e-commerce*.

E-commerce Buying and selling products with digital cash, via Electronic Data Interchange (EDI) or using *SSL* technologies to handle credit card transactions.

E-mail Electronic mail, the transmission of messages over telecommunications networks. Some e-mail systems are confined to a single network, say within a company or a university, but others have gateways to other systems, enabling users to send messages anywhere. Most e-mail systems include a text editor for composing messages, which can be sent to a recipient's e-mail address or to several users at once. This is called broadcasting. At its worst, it is *spam*.

E-zine Electronic magazine, a web site designed like a printed magazine. Some e-zines are electronic versions of existing magazines, but others exist only in their digital format. Most e-zines are supported by advertisements but some charge a subscription.

FAQs Frequently Asked Questions, a hypertext document, help file or web page with answers to common questions about some topic.

Favorites The Internet Explorer version of *Bookmarks*. See also Appendix.

Filter This can refer to a program which allows or prevents certain information reaching the browser – examples are Cybersitter or Net Nanny (pages 104–105) which prevent children accessing some areas of the web. Also, in graphics programs and image editors a filter is an effect applied to an image, like a lens filter alters the look of a photograph.

Freeware Copyrighted software given away free by the author, usually allowing others to use the software and pass it on, but not sell it. See page 29.

Frequently Asked Questions See *FAQs*.

gif Graphics interchange format, one of two bit-mapped graphics formats (the other is *jpeg*) used in web pages. It supports colour and various resolutions and includes data compression, interlacing, transparency and other features which make it useful for computer-generated images.

Graphics Refers to a device or program which enables a computer to display and manipulate images, such as a graphics card or graphics package (an image editing and creating program).

Graphics interchange format See *gif*.

Hacking Altering a program, usually in an unauthorised way and often to get around a password, by changing the programming code directly.

Hits The retrieval of a page or an image from a web *server*, often presented as visitor numbers in a Hit Counter. Hits often are a misleading indication of *traffic* since calling up a web page with a graphic would count as two hits.

Home page The main page of a web site, an index, table of contents, welcome page or password box.

Host A computer system (or its owner) which contains the data to be accessed by remote computer systems. Many companies host web *servers* – they provide the hardware, software and communications required by the server, but the content on the server can be provided and *uploaded* by others.

HTML Hypertext Markup Language, the agreed standard for describing the contents and appearance of pages on the web.

Icon A small picture that represents an *object* or a program.

Interface Anything which allows connection. For instance, Windows is a graphical user interface (GUI) which allows a user to connect with the computer.

Internet service provider A company or service which provides access to the internet and usually provides a username, password and *dial-up* phone number, plus the software to use these. ISPs (also called IAPs or Internet Access Providers) are connected to one another through Network Access Points (NAPs).

IP address See *domain name.*

ISP See *internet service provider.*

Java A high-level, platform-independent programming language developed by Sun Microsystems. Originally designed for hand-held devices and set-top boxes, it was modified in 1995 to take advantage of the need to create executable content within web pages. Java is an object-oriented language similar to C++, but simplified to remove features that cause common programming errors. Java interpreters known as Java Virtual Machines exist for most operating systems, so Java can run on most operating systems including UNIX, Macintosh and Windows. Small Java applications (*applets*) can be downloaded from a web server and run on your computer by a Java-compatible browser, such as Netscape or Internet Explorer. Some pundits predict that the software sales industry is under threat, because soon all applications will be in the form of applets, downloaded as required.

JavaScript Based on *Java*, this Netscape scripting language can integrate *HTML, plug-ins* and Java *applets* to each other

Joint photographic experts group See *jpeg.*

jpeg A graphical file format, like *gif,* used to display high-resolution images on the web. It has user-specified compression which can significantly reduce file sizes to about 5 per cent of the original (an advantage when *downloading*), although detail is lost in the compression. It is especially good for photo-realistic colour images. Files have the extension .jpg.

jpg See *jpeg.*

Link In hypertext systems, such as the web, a link is a reference to another page or object which the user can visit when the link is clicked.

Log on To make a computer system or network recognise the user, usually by entering a username and/or password. Also called log in and login.

Meta tags System meta variables, HTML tags which provides information about a web page or site but which do not affect how the page is displayed. Usually they hold information such as author, title, what the page is about, and keywords which indicate content. Many *search engines* use this information.

Mirror site A replica of another web site, used to reduce network *traffic* (*hits*) on a server or improve the availability of the site. This is useful when the original site generates too much traffic for a single server. Mirror sites can also increase the speed of access – a US-based web site mirrored in Sweden, say, will improve European users' access. Heavily used sites many have many mirrors in strategic locations worldwide.

Multimedia The integrated presentation of text, graphics, sound, video and animation. Multimedia applications were uncommon until increases in performance and decreases in hardware prices made it possible for all PCs to display video and play decent sound. Because multimedia applications are large, they are usually stored and distributed on CD-ROM.

Navigation Finding the contents of a web site. Good sites have simple, obvious and intuitive navigation.

Newbie A new user on an on-line service, particularly the web.

Newsgroup An on-line forum or discussion group. There are tens of thousands of newsgroups on the web, catering for every interest. To read and send newsgroup messages, you will need a news reader, a program which connects your PC to a news server. (See page 51.)

Object Any item which can be individually manipulated, including images but also other kinds of software entities such as data and procedures to handle the data. A spreadsheet or a *button* could be an object within a web page, for example.

Off-line Not connected. A web page or e-mail message can be downloaded for off-line (i.e. local) reading later. See *On-line*.

On-line Connected. Users are on-line when they are connected to a web service by a modem or network. Also used as one word (online).

PDF Portable Document Format. See *Adobe Acrobat*.

PICS See *RSAC*.

Plug-ins Software which integrates *multimedia* (sound, video, etc.) and certain interactive capabilities into web browsers, especially Netscape. See *ActiveX*.

Portal A web site or service offering a range of resources such as *e-mail*, *newsgroups*, *search engines*, *links* and on-line shopping opportunities. The first portals were on-line services such as Compuserve which provided access to the web via a specially designed *interface*. Now most search engines (AltaVista, Lycos, etc.) have become portals in an attempt to get and keep an audience who use them as their point of contact with the web.

RSAC The Recreational Software Advisory Council, established to provide ratings for web and internet content. It uses the Platform for Internet Content Selection (PICS) infrastructure to provide ratings on sites. See page 105.

rtf Rich Text Format, a word processing standard developed by Microsoft for specifying formatting of documents independent of the software package, making transfer of documents between packages (Word, Notepad, AmiPro) easier.

SCAM The real definition is an acronym for SCSI Configuration Automatically, a subset of the PnP specification that provides plug-and-play support for SCSI devices. But to most of us it is the practice of appearing to offer something in a web site (free software, interesting pictures, the chance to make a million, etc.) that isn't really there.

Search engine A database and the associated programming which allows web sites to be searched and found using a *spider*. Almost 75 per cent of *traffic* to most web sites comes from the 10 major search engines, including Infoseek, Lycos, Excite, WebCrawler, AltaVista and Hotbot.

Server A computer which provides services on a network and actually holds the web sites. Also called a *host*.

Shareware Software distributed free of charge, but with a small fee if you intend to use it. Usually registration provides support and updates. Shareware is cheap because it is usually offered directly to the customer by *downloading*, so there is little production, packaging or marketing cost. Shareware is not public-domain software or *freeware*.

Spam Electronic junk mail or newsgroup postings. Some people define it as any unsolicited e-mail, usually advertising sent to a mailing list or newsgroup. It is unpopular because it is unwanted and can clog up a server.

Spider A program that automatically fetches web pages to a *search engine*. When it finds a link in a web page it fetches the other page. Also called a webcrawler.

SSL Secure Sockets Layer, a protocol developed by Netscape for sending documents securely over the internet. SSL uses a private key to encrypt data. Many web sites now use SSL to handle confidential user information like credit card numbers. Web pages that require SSL usually start with https:// instead of http://.

Surfing Undirected web *browsing*, as opposed to searching for specific information.

Traffic The activity on a communications system, or the number of *hits* to a web site or page.

Uniform resource locator See *URL*.

Upload See *download*.

URL The 'name' of a web site, such as http://www.fifeweb.net/

USENET A worldwide *bulletin board* system that can be accessed through the web or other on-line service. USENET has more than 15,000 forums called *newsgroups* and is accessed by millions of people daily all over the world.

Version 4 browser Any version of Netscape Navigator or Netscape Communicator above Version 4.0 and any version of Internet Explorer above Version 4. By a coincidence, Netscape brought out Netscape Communicator 4.0 around the same time as Internet Explorer 4.0, both of which had added functionality, such as the ability to run Java, Dynamic HTML and ActiveX. See page 98.

Virus A program or piece of code loaded onto a computer without the user's knowledge, often carried with another program. Most viruses can replicate – make a copy over and over again – which will soon use all available memory and hang the system. Some viruses can transmit themselves across networks and overcome security systems. A worm is a type of virus which can replicate itself and use up memory, but does not attach itself to other programs. See page 98 for anti-virus software.

VRML Virtual Reality Modelling Language, a specification for displaying three-dimensional objects on the world wide web. VRML files have a .wrl (short for world) extension. To view these files, you need a VRML browser or a VRML plug-in to a web browser. See page 33.

Web browser See *browser*.

Web cam Or webcam – a video camera which sends images to a web page. See page 181.

Web ring Virtual communities of web sites with linked *navigation*, usually free of charge to visitors and members but carrying paid advertising. See page 91.

Winsock Short for Windows Socket, an Application Programming Interface (API) for developing Windows programs that can communicate with other machines using the TCP/IP protocol. Windows 95 and /NT comes with Dynamic Link Library (DLL) called winsock.dll.

Wizard A helper utility in an application that leads the user through the steps of a process, such as installing software.

Zip file File compressed with the ZIP format, which unzips to one or more files. This is not to be confused with the zip drive, a high-capacity drive developed by Iomega Corporation. Zip disks are slightly larger and thicker than floppy disks but can hold 100 Mb of data, useful for backing up hard disks and for transporting large files.

More computer and internet definitions are available on-line at http://webopedia.internet.com/.

Bookmarks (Netscape) and Favorites (Internet Explorer)

Bookmarks in Netscape Navigator, and Favorites in Internet Explorer are a good way to organise links to web pages you visit frequently or want to visit again. Some bookmarks and favorites came with your browser, selected by Netscape or Microsoft. You can change, delete, rearrange and add to these.

WORKING WITH BOOKMARKS (NETSCAPE)

How to bookmark a web page
1. Make sure your browser is showing the location toolbar at the top (View, Show, Location Toolbar) – the Bookmarks icon should be to the left of the Location box.
2. Access the web page you want to bookmark.
3. Click Bookmarks and choose Add Bookmark. The current web page is added to the end of the Bookmark menu.

How to open a bookmarked web page
1. Click Bookmarks.
2. Move your mouse cursor over a bookmarked folder (in which case another sub-menu will open) or page.
3. Left-click to access that page.

How to organise your bookmarks
To change the order of bookmarks:
Click Bookmarks and choose Edit Bookmarks. Click and drag any bookmark, folder or separator to another position it. You can also drag and drop page bookmarks into folders.

Note: There is no easy way to organise bookmarks alphabetically, not even by using View by Name, which is perverse.

To delete a bookmark:
Click Bookmarks and choose Edit Bookmarks. Click on any bookmark and:
- press the Delete key *or*
- click on Edit, Delete *or*
- right-click and Delete Bookmark.

To add a new folder:
Click Bookmarks and choose Edit Bookmarks. Click just above the position where you want the new folder. File New Folder or right-click and choose New Folder. Type the name of your new folder in Bookmark

Properties, and any comments (date, memos, etc.) in the large white box. Click OK to finish.

How to choose the folder for new bookmarks
1. Click Bookmarks and choose Edit Bookmarks.
2. Put the mouse cursor over the folder you want and click View, Set as New Bookmarks Folder.

How to search for bookmarks
1. Click Bookmarks and choose Edit Bookmarks.
2. In the Edit menu, choose Find in Bookmarks.
3. Type in any text you want to find in the bookmark titles. You can narrow the search to Name (the label which appears in the bookmark menu), Location (the URL) or Description (text typed into the description box when the bookmark was created using New) or a combination of these.
4. Click OK.

How to use multiple bookmark files
You can have more than one bookmark list, but only one bookmark list can be active at a time. This is useful if each family member or PC user wants individual bookmarks, or if you need separate bookmark lists for different jobs. This book, for instance, was initially created as a new bookmark list with the name and URL of each chosen site entered as a new bookmark and the textual description added as I explored the web site in question. This was later turned into a text document (see below).

Save the current bookmark file:
Click Bookmarks and choose Edit Bookmarks. Click on File Save As. Choose a suitable location. The list is saved in HTML format and bookmark.htm is the default. Be careful not to overwrite the default file. Choose a new name for it, like mybookmark.htm.

Create a new bookmark file:
The easiest way is to open Notepad and use File, Save As to save the empty file wherever you choose as something.htm, remembering to use the Save as, Save as type, All Files (*.*) option.
Open the Edit Bookmarks menu, click File, Open Bookmarks File and find your new file.

Note: This file can also be opened in your browser. Try it – it looks very different.

How to update your bookmarks
1. When you are on-line, click Bookmarks and choose Edit Bookmarks.
2. Select one or more bookmarks. To check all bookmarks, do not select any.
3. Click on View, Update Bookmarks.

4. Select All Bookmarks or Selected Bookmarks and click on Start Checking. If a page has changed, Netscape marks the bookmark icon. If it cannot verify a change, a question mark appears on the bookmark's icon. This is useful for checking whether the contents of a site have changed since you last browsed it.

How to change details of a bookmark or folder
1. Click Bookmarks and choose Edit Bookmarks.
2. Select a bookmark or folder.
3. Click on Edit, Bookmark Properties. This opens the same dialogue box as in *To add a new folder* (above).
4. Click OK to save this.

How to create a shortcut
You may wish to have a shortcut icon on your desktop or in a desktop window which can launch the browser and open a particular page right away. There are three ways to achieve this.

Create a shortcut from a link:
Click and drag a link in a web page to the desktop and release the mouse button.

Create a shortcut for the current web page:
Click and drag the bookmark icon from the bookmark menu to your desktop.

Create a shortcut using the bookmark:
Click on Bookmarks and Edit Bookmarks. Click and drag the bookmark you want to your desktop.

WORKING WITH FAVORITES (INTERNET EXPLORER)
How to add a page to your list of favorites (note the American spelling)
1. Browse the page you want to add to your Favourites list.
2. Click on Favorites menu, click Add to Favorites.
3. Type a name for the page or choose the one given.
4. If you do not see a list of folders below this, click the Create in button.
5. Click on the folder where you want your new Favorite to be placed.
6. Click on OK to save it.

How to make a favorite available off-line
This is useful if you refer to a web page often but do not want to go on-line each time.
1. Click on Favorites Organize Favorites.
2. Click the page you want to make available off-line.
3. Check Make available off-line. This saves the page locally on your PC. The Properties button will now appear. You may alter a number of properties,

including the schedule for updating the page, how much to download and the nature of synchronisation with the on-line page. For instance, you could set it to synchronise every time you go on-line, even if you do not actually browse that page or site.

4. While on-line, click on Tools, Synchronize.

How to organise your favorites
1. Click on Favorites, Organize Favorites.
2. Click Create Folder, give a name for the folder, and either press your keyboard ENTER button or click Close.
3. If the favorites window is still open, click and drag shortcuts or folders into other folders.
4. Alternatively, mark a folder or favorite icon and click the **Move to Folder** button.

Note: This procedure can make Explorer 5 crash and close.

How to share bookmarks and folders
Sharing between Internet Explorer and Netscape
Internet Explorer can automatically import your Netscape bookmarks.
1. Click on File, Import and Export and an Import/Export Wizard will open.
2. Follow the instructions, choosing the Import Favorites option and give the location of your Netscape bookmark file.
3. Choose a folder to save them in.

Sharing between Netscape and Internet Explorer
1. Start with Internet Explorer. Click on File, Import and Export and the Import/Export Wizard will open.
2. Follow the instructions and this time choose the Export Favorites option.
3. Choose a name and location for a Netscape bookmark file, remembering not to overwrite any existing bookmark file.
4. Open Netscape, click on Bookmarks, Edit Bookmarks, File, Import.
5. Choose the file you created with the Explorer Export Wizard and click on Open.

Sharing between PCs
If you use Internet Explorer or Netscape on different PCs, you can share favorites and bookmarks between them by saving or exporting the files to a floppy disk and importing them on another PC. They can also be sent to other users as e-mail attachments.

HINT: if you use both Internet Explorer and Navigator, keep your favorites and bookmarks up-to-date with each other by importing them between programs on a regular basis.

INDEX OF WEB SITES

This index is arranged alphabetically by nickname (Acrobat before Actinic Software) ignoring any initial 'The' in the title.

INDEX OF WEB SITES